P9-CMD-251

Managing Projects in Trouble

Achieving Turnaround and Success

PROJECT MANAGEMENT TITLES
FROM AUERBACH PUBLICATIONS AND CRC PRESS

Managing Web Projects
Edward B. Farkas
ISBN: 978-1-4398-0495-7

**The Complete Project Management
Methodology and Toolkit**
Gerard M. Hill
ISBN: 978-1-4398-0154-3

**Implementing Program Management:
Templates and Forms Aligned with the**
Standard for Program Management —
Second Edition (2008)
Ginger Levin and Allen M. Green
ISBN: 978-1-4398-1605-9

Project Management Recipes for Success
Guy L. De Furia
ISBN: 978-1-4200-7824-4

**Project Management of Complex and
Embedded Systems: Ensuring Product
Integrity and Program Quality**
Kim H. Pries and Jon Quigley
ISBN: 978-1-4200-7205-1

**Leading IT Projects: The IT
Manager's Guide**
Jessica Keyes
ISBN: 978-1-4200-7082-8

**Building a Project Work Breakdown
Structure: Visualizing Objectives,
Deliverables, Activities, and Schedules**
Dennis P. Miller
ISBN: 978-1-4200-6969-3

**A Standard for Enterprise
Project Management**
Michael S. Zambruski
ISBN: 978-1-4200-7245-7

Global Engineering Project Management
M. Kemal Atesmen
ISBN: 978-1-4200-7393-5

**Effective Communications for
Project Management**
Ralph L. Kliem
ISBN: 978-1-4200-6246-5

Managing Global Development Risk
James M. Hussey and Steven E. Hall
ISBN: 978-1-4200-5520-7

**The Strategic Project Leader: Mastering
Service-Based Project Leadership**
Jack Ferraro
ISBN: 978-0-8493-8794-4

Determining Project Requirements
Hans Jonasson
ISBN: 978-1-4200-4502-4

Practical Guide to Project Planning
Ricardo Viana Vargas
ISBN: 978-1-4200-4504-8

**The Complete Project Management
Office Handbook, Second Edition**
Gerard M. Hill
ISBN: 978-1-4200-4680-9

**Staffing the Project Office for
Competitive Advantage**
J. Kent Crawford
ISBN: 978-0-8247-5477-8

**Project Management Maturity Model,
Second Edition**
J. Kent Crawford
ISBN: 978-0-8493-7945-1

**Optimizing Human Capital with
a Strategic Project Office: Select,
Train, Measure, and Reward People
for Organization Success**
J. Kent Crawford and
Jeannette Cabanis-Brewin
ISBN: 978-0-8493-5410-6

Managing Projects in Trouble

Achieving Turnaround and Success

Ralph L. Kliem, PMP

CRC Press
Taylor & Francis Group
Boca Raton London New York

CRC Press is an imprint of the
Taylor & Francis Group, an **informa** business
AN AUERBACH BOOK

Auerbach Publications
Taylor & Francis Group
6000 Broken Sound Parkway NW, Suite 300
Boca Raton, FL 33487-2742

© 2011 by Taylor and Francis Group, LLC
Auerbach Publications is an imprint of Taylor & Francis Group, an Informa business

No claim to original U.S. Government works

Printed in the United States of America on acid-free paper
10 9 8 7 6 5 4 3 2 1

International Standard Book Number: 978-1-4398-5246-0 (Hardback)

This book contains information obtained from authentic and highly regarded sources. Reasonable efforts have been made to publish reliable data and information, but the author and publisher cannot assume responsibility for the validity of all materials or the consequences of their use. The authors and publishers have attempted to trace the copyright holders of all material reproduced in this publication and apologize to copyright holders if permission to publish in this form has not been obtained. If any copyright material has not been acknowledged please write and let us know so we may rectify in any future reprint.

Except as permitted under U.S. Copyright Law, no part of this book may be reprinted, reproduced, transmitted, or utilized in any form by any electronic, mechanical, or other means, now known or hereafter invented, including photocopying, microfilming, and recording, or in any information storage or retrieval system, without written permission from the publishers.

For permission to photocopy or use material electronically from this work, please access www.copyright.com (http://www.copyright.com/) or contact the Copyright Clearance Center, Inc. (CCC), 222 Rosewood Drive, Danvers, MA 01923, 978-750-8400. CCC is a not-for-profit organization that provides licenses and registration for a variety of users. For organizations that have been granted a photocopy license by the CCC, a separate system of payment has been arranged.

Trademark Notice: Product or corporate names may be trademarks or registered trademarks, and are used only for identification and explanation without intent to infringe.

Visit the Taylor & Francis Web site at
http://www.taylorandfrancis.com

and the Auerbach Web site at
http://www.auerbach-publications.com

ACC LIBRARY SERVICES AUSTIN, TX

For Tonia and Mulder

Contents

List of Figures

Preface

Projects have a high fatality rate. Like salmon swimming upstream, more die than live. For each failure, what follows is usually a legacy of anger, hurt, frustration, finger pointing, infighting, and sometimes worse. Even if a project partially succeeds, that is, it meets some of its objectives, the consequences can be severe.

During my 25 years plus in the "fog" of project management in a corporate environment, I have managed to survive many projects, even one or two on the brink of failure. I have also been brought on board to turn around projects deemed as being in trouble. Based upon my knowledge and experience, I have discovered five key secrets to turn around the most difficult project.

Of course, these five secrets did not come easily. I had to work to master each one through trial and error with varying degrees of success. And I can tell you right now, you will have to go through several experiences before you can truly say you can effectively turn around a project in trouble with a fair degree of confidence.

In this book, I am sharing these five secrets to help you better manage your projects in general, and troubled ones, so that you don't feel as if you're taking a pleasure cruise on the Titanic or Lusitania.

In the Army, we were always told that the best way to deal with an artillery barrage was to go through it. You don't stop in your tracks because the rounds will bombard you to death. You don't retreat because the enemy will adjust their sights and fire for effect as you leave or wait there to ambush you. What you do is move forward, making progress until you reach your destination. The key is to reach your destination in a way that maximizes your gain and minimizes your losses. Unfortunately, too, many project managers manage a project in trouble that minimizes gains and maximizes losses.

While the five key actions for maximizing gains and minimizing losses you will learn from this book may seem like common sense, it has been quite clear from my perspective that the common sense described here is really not that common. Rather, it is quite rare as you will find by reading on. At the end of each chapter, starting with the heading Energize, there will be a checklist that you can use to help you turn around your project.

Also, at the end of each chapter, starting with the Introduction, you will read an actual case study about a project that implemented these actions and steps described in the book; only the company and individual names have been changed.

If you're a project management professional and have not experienced a project in trouble to any degree, you have my admiration. However, I will venture to guess that if that is the case, you haven't had much exposure to a variety of projects in different environments; the projects have not been that complex or challenging; or you've simply not been placed in a position to turn a project around.

Whatever the reason, I highly recommend that you learn the five actions for turning around projects in trouble.

Or, continue what you're doing at your own peril!

Ralph Kliem, MA, PMP, ABCP
LeanPM, LLC
www.theleanpm.com
Ralph@theleanpm.com

1

Introduction

Think about this scenario. You've just been assigned as the project manager of a project that has the reputation of being an unmitigated disaster. Management does not want to cancel the project. So, the big question is, what do you do?

If you're like most people, you're standing still like a deer in the middle of the road and staring right into the headlights of an oncoming vehicle. The choices are to stay put or flee. Either way, the results are not good. Stay, and you become roadkill. Run away, and you may get hit by another oncoming vehicle in the other lane, fall off a cliff, or get eaten by wolves.

So, you are faced with a dilemma. Stay put or run? Many people decide to run. They take their chances by putting together a resume and hope for the best elsewhere. A few decide to stay put and face another existential decision: allow themselves to become victims or take action.

What would be your decision?

1.1 WHAT YOU'LL LEARN

In this book, you will learn to take action in a way that will increase the likelihood of success and minimize the possibility of failure for you and your project.

Specifically, you will be able to

- Recognize the symptoms of troubled projects.
- Make the necessary changes to turn around projects in trouble.
- Revisit a project's vision, and develop a new or revised vision.
- Look at all the options to turn a project into reality.
- Choose the most appropriate option.
- Execute the new or revised vision.

1.2 THE ODDS ARE AGAINST YOU

The odds are high that you already have inherited or will inherit a project in trouble. The studies substantiating this fact are quite numerous and plentiful. That's often because the conditions—despite the advancements in project management—are conducive to project failure.

Whether you use budget, schedule, quality, or some other criterion, the statistics by think tanks, institutes, associations, and other trade organizations all point to one inescapable conclusion: A project has a greater chance of getting into trouble than staying out of it.

The context of a project can be quite complicated. The interplay of a host of variables can influence a project's outcome.

Strategic objectives, corporate values, team mores, management styles, policies, methods, tool availability, team member attitudes, and expertise are just a few of the contextual factors that can affect the state of a project.

Projects in general and project managers in particular face many pressures, too. These pressures can originate from various levels and organizations that a project must deal with throughout its life cycle. This includes politics, reviews and approvals, legal compliance, marketing environment, procurement sources, and much more.

On top of all that, projects must deal with issues on an increasingly larger scale in terms of size and complexity. These issues include outsourcing, virtual teaming, globalization, and compliance.

The conclusion? The chances of a project getting into trouble keep increasing. It seems every solution brings with it a greater level of complexity, which project managers will have to handle. With this greater level of complexity comes the correspondingly greater chances for projects and their project managers to get into trouble.

1.3 SYMPTOMS TO LOOK FOR

Despite the odds, many managers and project managers seem oblivious to the symptoms of troubled projects. These symptoms are quite ubiquitous and obvious, yet many choose to ignore and not address them.

1.3.1 Poorly Defined and Managed Scope and Requirements

It is amazing how many projects are initiated without an understanding of what it is all about. Instead, the project takes off like an airplane without a destination. Gradually, it evolves into something whose end result not even the key people understand. Ask a simple question such as, what are the project's goals and objectives? What is in and out of scope? What are the specific requirements that the project must address? The chances are negligible that anyone will be able to give you a direct answer to such questions; in all probability, they will take umbrage at you for asking them such questions in the first place.

1.3.2 Lack of Involvement and Buy-In of Key Stakeholders

Many projects pop up out of nowhere. They are like atolls in the middle of the Pacific; they have very few, if any, "inhabitants"; they lie low, and nobody wants to go to them.

For example, it is amazing how many projects exist under the assumption that "if you build it they will come." Take a typical large project involving millions of dollars. Ask a simple question such as "Who is the customer?" and don't be surprised if you get a perplexed look or incoherent mumbling. Granted, sometimes projects are so complex that there are many different types of customers. But customers must be identified, to give you an idea of whose needs you need to satisfy so as to be able to define them. Sometimes, to add another level of complexity and confusion, the person or organization you think is the customer is not really the customer, and the real answer emerges after the product or service has been delivered and, frequently, not in a positive way.

Now take this line of thinking one step further, and you'll likely find that the people or organizations you thought were interested in the project are, in truth, not interested. They may have attended meetings, but the reality is that they are socialites who are everyone's favorite houseguests; nobody knows why they show up at meetings. Or they claim they represent a key stakeholder but have absolutely no substantive background about the person or organization they represent.

1.3.3 Lack of Detail and Realism in the Project Plan

Many projects in trouble have a plan, or something that existing participants call a plan. More often than not, the plan has a few milestones with a sizable percentage of them marked TBD, To Be Determined. Coupled with this is a lack of detail or realistic analysis of how the milestone was determined other than some high-level executive or manager licking the tip of his or her finger and plucking a milestone date out of midair. Just about everyone shakes their heads like bobbleheads with the hope that the project will or that they can find another opportunity elsewhere.

Often, the history and assumptions behind the schedule are known only to a few. If some people leave, then what often happens is that the schedule either gets ignored or it does not give a true picture of what is happening; either way, the schedule is of no use to anyone.

1.3.4 Negative Conflicts among Team Members and Poor Morale

One of the key signs of projects in trouble is the dynamics among the team members and their relationships with other stakeholders. In just about any project facing difficulties—whatever the reasons—the quality of the relationships is key. Just a few toxic relationships can affect the entire performance of a project, have harmful effects on people and, consequently, degrade the overall results achieved.

Toxic personalities and their relationships with others are perhaps the most difficult part of turning around a project in trouble. Too many of them are allowed to continue out of fear, denial, and legal concerns. Yet, it is often more costly to not deal with these personalities and their relationships than to take them head-on.

Their impact is undeniable. These people inhibit thinking and communications. Morale sinks. Teaming fails. Sabotage can occur, and anger may lurk below the surface, waiting to erupt at any moment.

It is certain that the most significant contributors to poor project performance are related to this scenario. Constrained resources, compressed schedules, shifting priorities, and countless other situations may cause conflict, but they are just enablers that toxic personalities capitalize on. The history of projects is replete with examples in which constrained resources and compressed timetables seemed insurmountable and yet the teams still succeeded. History is also replete with project teams that enjoyed every conceivable advantage, but where toxic team members and relationships contributed immensely to project failure.

1.3.5 Ill-Defined Assumptions and Expectations

Assumptions are nothing more than facts assumed to be real or imagined. Expectations are what people assume will be the results of their efforts. Amazingly, projects large and small alike operate on assumptions and expectations that few people even question, document, or articulate. Many projects get into trouble because key stakeholders never question their assumptions or the expectations of others. Instead, many projects chug along with everyone thinking that everything is fine until something "hits the fan"—and it isn't air. For example, few projects start off with a listing of assumptions that serve as the basis for making key decisions and developing plans. Few project managers make any effort to identify success criteria for the customer. The result is often high rework and recovery costs, which not only increase overhead costs but also eat up the managerial gains anticipated for the project in the first place.

There are many reasons why projects proceed without a common understanding, let alone questioning of expectations. Some people simply go along with the flow. Others prefer to operate in a veil of ignorance. Still others are there for their paycheck. Others just want to avoid the pain of asking about it in the first place. After a while, the assumptions and expectations are treated as a given until the very end, when the results of the projects demonstrate that the assumptions were incorrect and the expectations (if they exist at all) are unrealistic.

1.3.6 Lack of People with the Necessary Attributes

Many projects in trouble have people with the necessary skills. Other projects have people who lack the necessary hard and soft skills.

Some people may have all the hard skills, for example, programming or data modeling expertise, but lack the soft ones to do the job, for example, effective listening, looking at different perspectives, etc. Or a person can have great soft skills but lack the expertise to do the necessary technical work to get the job done efficiently and effectively.

Of course, nobody is perfect, though many people think they are. A mismatch in skills—for example, a person on a critical path failing to perform up to expectations for whatever reason—can have devastating consequences for the overall performance of a project. It can also be devastating for the individual.

It is interesting to note that hard skills seem to have more relevance in the selection of people on a project team. Perhaps this is because the hard skills are more tangible, whereas the soft skills are less so. Many projects are in trouble, however, not because of a dearth of hard skills but soft skills. This is especially the case with technical projects where hard skills are necessary to accomplish the tangible work. Yet, many studies reveal that most of these projects fail not because of issues related to expertise in hard skills but with soft ones.

Hard versus soft skills aside, most projects in trouble have skills-related issues. Often, the prerequisite skills are not identified or are identified too late in the life cycle or the work breakdown structure or the responsibility assignment matrix is missing or incomplete. The incompleteness or lack of these two items is directly linked to the inability to determine what skills are necessary to start, continue, or conclude a project.

1.3.7 Failure to Identify or Deal with Risks

In many projects in trouble, risks are not addressed or, if they are, they are addressed at a high level. Most projects face risks, some of which are more challenging and critical than others. Some projects operate on the assumption—real or imagined—that everything will work out. The reality is that few projects ever work out as planned, especially if no effort is made to identify risks and, more importantly, take action to deal with them. Even if people recognize that risks exist, some may succumb to institutional or peer pressure to deny their existence. The failure to identify or deal with them may be the result of politics or groupthink. Whatever the cause, ignoring risks of all magnitude makes projects vulnerable to failure, perhaps not immediately but eventually. This failure to identify risks, in fact, may not surface during a project's life cycle but may do so much later during the product life cycle; this may be reflected, for example, in substantial maintenance costs.

People responsible for projects in trouble may have identified risks but elected to do nothing about them. The risks may appear at first rather inconsequential but later pop up as significant risks. The danger here is that failure to address a risk early makes it much more difficult to do so later on. That's because rework and costs will be greater, and any action may be too late.

A concomitant to not addressing risks is not to do so adequately up front. Instead, a band-aid approach is applied when a tourniquet is needed. This approach is fine if ongoing monitoring of risks and their mitigation occurs. However, projects in trouble often suffer from inadequate monitoring.

1.3.8 Too Many Dependencies

This symptom of projects in trouble is frequently overlooked. Projects often take on a life of their own, operating as though they are independent. The reality is that these projects often depend on the effectiveness of other organizations and projects for resources and deliverables. Projects in trouble frequently overlook these dependencies, assuming instead that they can operate independently. But no project is an island. Holding such a false belief is similar to inhabitants on an atoll believing tsunamis can't affect them.

For projects in trouble, these risks often are not cited in their assumptions or issues. Partly, the rationale is the feeling that nothing can be done about them and partly because there is an unrealistic belief that the project can be salvaged even under the most dreadful circumstances. Regardless of the reason, the failure to recognize external dependencies can lead to a feeling of invulnerability, in turn, leading to trouble if and when something does happen.

All of these symptoms manifest themselves as cost, schedule, and quality performance of a project. The costs of a project continue to force a project manager to request additional funding or tap the management reserves. The slides of milestones in the schedule lead to constant application of corrective actions and workarounds. The defective output can cause a stream of rework that, in turn, contributes to consumption of the budget ahead of the baseline and causes the schedule to slide.

The symptoms of projects in trouble are just a sample of the ones that ultimately lead to their dismal fate. Many project managers will likely ascertain one or more of the symptoms discussed and others subsequently described in this book. The key is to look for these symptoms and be able to determine the causes and effectively address them. Failure to do so only leads to history repeating itself. As the philosopher-historian Santayana noted, he who ignores history is destined to repeat it. A project manager with a project in trouble would be wise to heed Santayana's words.

1.4 PATTERNS TO LOOK FOR

Most projects in trouble exemplify one of three patterns that lead to problems.

Management by Crisis is the first pattern. Project managers find themselves constantly "behind the eight ball." It is one problem after another that gets attention and, more often than not, all problems are treated equally. Eventually, the project manager and his or her team members get tired addressing or fixing problems (often the same ones over and over), the number of problems mount, and the project falls even further behind in just about any criterion used as a basis to evaluate its success.

Nothing ever seems to get done, and if anything is, it is done as a short-term fix, not a permanent solution. The common failing leading to this pattern of behavior is not having a vision or having an inadequate vision for the project, which, in turn, leads to not having priorities, not having a defined scope, poor scheduling practices, escalating costs, and poor quality of output. Like a child with a hammer who sees everything as a nail, project managers with this pattern of performance view all problems or issues equally, dissipating energy and effort that rarely leads to a lasting, efficient, and effective delivery of a product or service.

Management by Drives is another typical pattern of behavior that can lead to a project in trouble.

Projects with this pattern often start off slowly and sometimes may start getting some momentum but do so gradually. Frequently, the project team does some exploratory work and becomes more of a committee than a team. Not much happens for a long time until the latter phases of a project, and then there is this mad rush to meet the deadline. It is akin to a college student who does little or no studying throughout the quarter or semester and crams the night prior to the exam.

The major contributor to this pattern of behavior is that not only is there a lack of leadership and self-discipline on the part of all the stakeholders but also a vague notion of what needs to be done. In other words, the vision, requirements, and success criteria have not been identified, or the identification has not been done at a sufficient level of detail. During the latter part of the project life cycle, a frantic attempt is made to get the work done. This effort often leads to greater overhead costs due to payment for overtime, producing marginal results at best (and often introducing errors), cutting back on key tasks, and pushing work into the future.

Naturally, a project with this pattern of behavior can't help but fall into trouble. The schedule slides, the cost escalates, and the quality of output declines. No one is content with the result.

The third pattern is *Management by Confusion*. This pattern reflects a project in total disarray. People scurry about like "chickens with their heads cut off." The leadership, if there is any at all, lacks control over the resources. Resources are wasted, goals and objectives are missed, people clash with one another, and esprit de corps is nonexistent. Turnover and absenteeism are common. In the end, no one is happy—not the project manager, not team members, not customers, not management.

The causes of this pattern are many. Leadership is weak, if it exists at all; lack of vision is the norm rather than the exception; poor scheduling practices are in place; no one follows any disciplined, standard approach to the work; visibility of the results, good or bad, does not occur; and productivity is low. In other words, efforts to achieve cost, schedule, and quality criteria leave much to be desired.

Ideally, projects should exhibit a pattern known as *Management by Effectiveness*. This pattern is reflected in project managers who know what the vision is, the path to achieve it, the resources required to execute it, the success criteria to determine successful performance, and who know how to track performance to determine whether success has been achieved. Typically, these project managers use all resources cost-effectively and keep tabs on whether results are meeting the expectations of the stakeholders. If something goes awry, these project managers exercise due diligence and due care to bring performance back in alignment with expectations.

Naturally, projects in trouble do not exhibit the pattern of Management by Effectiveness. These projects reflect either Management by Crisis, Management by Confusion, or Management by Drives. It is these three patterns that this book focuses on by providing a road map for turning them into projects Managed by Effectiveness.

1.5 THE FIVE KEY ACTIONS

There are five key actions for turning around projects in trouble, called the five E's: Energize, Envision, Explore, Evaluate, and Execute.

Energize is providing the spark for making change happen. The premise is that change will not occur unless someone motivates people to act. Without that spark, the project in trouble will continue to go downhill.

And what is the source of that spark? You, the project manager. You are the one who takes the first step to get people to move in a new direction. This spark can have the explosive effect of a big bang or the click of a cigarette lighter at a natural gas plant. The magnitude of the effect depends on the circumstances and your style and capabilities as a project manager.

Envision is revisiting the vision and developing a new or revised vision. When a project continues to face trouble, the likelihood is that the project vision is no longer relevant, is nonexistent, or is off-base partially or totally from what key stakeholders had originally intended. It is critical that a project have a solid vision of what is to be achieved because this provides the basis to develop subsequent plans and to make decisions throughout the project life cycle. A vague vision, or no vision, leads to inefficient and ineffective activities that inevitably lead to a project in trouble. It is critical, therefore, that a vision be clear, accurate, complete, and understandable to enable good project management throughout a project's life cycle.

Explore is looking for all the options that are available to execute the new or revised vision. These options may be major or minor, meaning they may span a whole replanning effort or simply involve making slight revisions to the vision for the project.

Regardless of the option, the key is to remain as objective and independent as possible when determining options. To act otherwise would open the way for a project to get in trouble once again in the future. The goal is to identify options that can lead to lasting, meaningful change so that a project does not get in trouble once again. Remember, the idea is to achieve Management by Effectiveness, and to achieve that is to identify options that further the new or revised vision. These options can take any form related to improving cost, schedule, and quality performance.

Evaluate is choosing the appropriate option. Like Explore, Evaluate should be as objective and independent as possible. In some cases, this should be even more objective and independent. Again, the idea is to embrace an option (or several options) for a lasting, meaningful change in the approach to a project. Once the option or options have been selected, there is one more step.

Execute is turning the vision and roadmap into reality. Here is where project managers and their teams apply all the relevant, adjusted-to-scale, project management tools, techniques, and disciplines. This not only includes

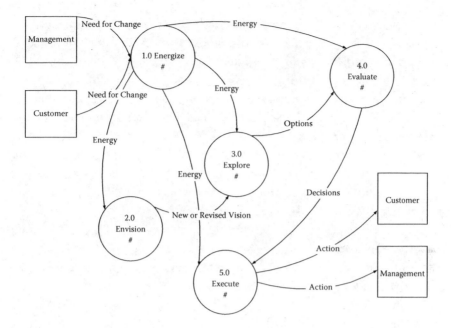

FIGURE 1.1
Level One: Overview of the five actions.

schedules but also other topics like status collection and assessment, change and configuration management, and communications management.

A discussion of the interaction of the five actions is shown in Figure 1.1.

One, the five key actions are nonlinear and nonsequential. However, they can occur linearly or sequentially, but that may not necessarily be the case. In many situations, these actions may occur concurrently, that is, at the same time, because they are interrelated and interdependent. Many project environments do not lend themselves to a sequential approach due to lack of time, money, or some other constraint.

Two, note that Energize is a critical action. The assumption here is that the project manager and the core team are the ones who initiate the need to act to turn around a project in trouble. This spark kick-starts a project into action, and other necessary actions are performed. The additional assumption is that nothing will change without exhibiting the necessary energy; otherwise, a project, like all systems, will either maintain equilibrium or run down.

One of the biggest dangers confronting a project manager when dealing with a project in trouble is to fail to take a holistic view of project management. Basically the project manager either sides with the art (i.e., the soft side), or the science (i.e., the hard side). Often, the latter predominates.

The art of project management depends on the right side of the brain. It is tied to the critical thinking aspects of the project, such as asking the question "Why are we doing this?" or "Is there a better way?" Examples of the art of project management include leadership, coaching, negotiating, motivating, and creative problem solving.

The science of project management deals with the left side of the brain. It is tied to applied thinking, such as applying a methodology and using a tool. The fundamental question is "How is this done?" Examples include schedule calculation and earned value.

A project needs both left-brain and right-brain thinking. Too often, however, the emphasis is on the science. This lopsided perspective can be the source of many problems that often center around people, communication, conflict, and much more.

To effectively energize a team into action, the science of project management needs to be an output of the art of project management. Project managers cannot disregard one without imperiling the other. Therefore, Energize relies heavily on the art of project management, so that a project manager can turn around the project.

Three, note that each action results in some output that feeds at least one other action or multiple actions. These outputs are often a transformation of inputs into some request, information, or signal that eventually feeds other actions.

Four, note that the kickoff and final ending points of the entire process are two entities: management and the customer. The assumption here is that the request for turning around a project in trouble is based on a decision made by management and the customer.

Also note that the actions all result in providing these same two entities, management and customer, with results. These results are twofold. The result for management is a new or revised approach to managing the project with the goal of achieving the success criteria related to cost, schedule, and quality. The other result is to the customer, and that is delivering a product or service that satisfies expectations or needs.

Here's an overall description of the approach to turning around a project in trouble; be advised that this is a sequential discussion, which in reality may not be the case.

Both management and the customer have concluded that a project is in trouble, for whatever reason; they have also decided that "killing," or terminating, the project is not an option. They have decided to reverse the project's fortunes by assigning a new project manager, you.

Right away, you need to energize the existing team, especially the core team, to change the way of doing business. This action will require collecting data and information and making various assessments.

Once your team has been energized, you can revisit the project's vision. This entails looking at the current vision (if one exists), taking a global perspective of what's happening, and diving into more details about what has and has not happened. You and your core team can then develop a new or revised vision for the project. This vision is based on the consensus of key stakeholders, such as the core team, key management, and the customer. With a good vision in place, the groundwork has been established for the other actions that need to be performed.

The next action is to Explore. The whole idea here is that you and your core team find out what aspects of the new or revised vision have been achieved and what aspects need correction or improvement. It entails collecting additional facts and data, obtaining ideas from others, and determining what activities add value to the attainment of the vision. The key is to capitalize on the resources available to you right now to develop a meaningful, reliable new approach to executing the project. This action includes developing one or more options for doing so.

After Exploring, the next action is to use information and data to evaluate the options for improvement. This action involves looking at the pros and cons of each option, which includes looking at the risks. The key here is to remain as objective as possible while at the same time maintaining a global perspective of the project. The options chosen will be what will lead to improving project performance to achieve a new or revised vision for the project.

The final action is to Execute. This action involves applying the project management disciplines, tools, and techniques to make the new or revised vision and selected options a reality. This entails activities like developing or revising a work breakdown structure, schedule, responsibility assignments, risk management, change management, and much more. The keys here are to implement the necessary changes with the participation of the team.

Note that the final results are then shared with management and the customer. This sharing includes their review and approval of everything deemed critical to the success of the project.

1.6 AVOID THE QUICK FIX

It is important to reiterate that although the actions are discussed sequentially, the reality is that they can occur concurrently to various degrees. This is especially the case when time for recovery is compressed. At no time, however, does this mean that project managers or the core team should go for the "quick fix" without realizing the downstream consequences of their decisions. The key is to develop a lasting, meaningful turnaround of a project in trouble.

Case Study

Background. Build the Best Systems Inc. (BSI) is a major application development firm, specializing in developing applications for the banking industry. Located in Portland, Oregon, the firm has gained a reputation for delivering the best applications in the business according to budget and on schedule.

But, for the first time, a major application development project has run into trouble. The internal customer, who is responsible for delivering the application to Large International Bank Inc. (LIBI) in New York, is extremely unhappy with the current state of the project. If the project continues in its current state, the project will exceed its budget by 50%, and the application will deliver a third of the functionality promised in the contract and the statement of work. BSI fears that if the project continues in the current way, it will lose money for the first time, and its reputation in the banking community will be tarnished. The budget for the project is $5 million, but is now projected to cost $7.5 million.

The accounting application is unique because it pulls data from a number of legacy systems at LIBI. The hope at BSI is that if this concept works for LIBI, then it can capitalize on the lessons learned and apply its approach to developing more applications for other institutions in the industry and get opportunities to do similar work in other industries.

The core team consists of twelve people and an extended team of twenty people. The core team consists of a project manager, system architect, database analyst, functional analysts, application developers, and an internal customer representative. While the team supports other projects, the current one is top priority according to the portfolio for BSI.

The current project manager, Harold, reports to a manager, Fred, in charge of accounting application development. Harold also acts as the system architect for the project, giving preference to technical considerations over project management. Hence, there are few project management disciplines in place; Harold basically runs meetings and sets milestones without consulting with the internal customer; and most effort is driven by technical problems, to which the team reacts rather than responds. The customer has expressed displeasure with the results, both from a technical and project management perspective, yet nothing seems to change. Periodic reports to LIBI have been high level, basically stating that good progress is being made and the major milestone date will be met. There has been no mention of the rework, delivery failures, missed milestones, or budget overruns that have occurred internally on the project.

Fred and his management are getting frustrated with Harold's performance. In addition to having an abrasive, intimidating personality who describes himself as "your worst nightmare," Harold has maneuvered himself into a position that makes it difficult for Fred to turn circumstances around for two reasons: many of the team members fear him, and Fred is convinced that he needs Harold's expertise. Meanwhile, the entire team finds itself suffering from high turnover, low morale, no teaming, mistrust, no customer involvement, and unstable scope. Just to deliver something that will meet any major internal milestone, low periods of seemingly no work done occur, and then there is a mad rush to deliver something to the customer to allay concerns, knowing that the output does not meet expectations because requirements are ill-defined and because any problems can be handled through rework. Besides, milestones in the current schedule have slid so many times that the customer no longer has any faith in the published schedule.

In desperation, Fred decided to hire a new project manager while retaining Harold as the system architect. Harold was not happy when Deborah came on board as the new project manager.

2

Energize

2.1 THE SPARK

Energize, Figure 2.1, is the first key action, whose overall purpose is to motivate the existing team members to recognize that a need exists for change and that it cannot happen without their support.

There are some benefits gained by performing this action. They are

- Accepting that the past has not worked
- Acknowledging that change is necessary
- Recognizing that they are not helpless victims and have control over their destiny
- Overcoming fear
- Understanding of a project's circumstances

Acceptance of the fact that the past has not worked is not easy. Change is difficult at all levels, from the individual to the group level. Change, however, is not impossible. For change to occur people must acknowledge that it is necessary and beneficial.

On projects, change is a way of life because a project is in a state of constant flux, going from Point A to Point Z. Some people on a project can view change negatively because it impacts them personally, psychologically, physiologically, and professionally. One of the biggest negative roadblocks is the admission that what has been done in the past was incorrect, irrelevant, unnecessary, or poor. From a project perspective, this assessment usually comes from management and the customer alike.

This assessment is hard to accept because people have invested emotionally in the project, and now management and the customer have decided on the need for change as an expression of dissatisfaction with performance.

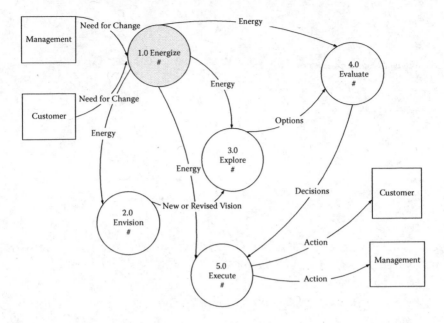

FIGURE 2.1
Level One Overview: Energize.

Egos get bruised, often leading to finger-pointing or withdrawal or both, resulting in the problems facing the project going into a spiral.

Energizing enables you to take these issues head-on, from psychological, sociological, and process perspectives. Like a person with a drug problem, the first step is to acknowledge that a problem exists and recovery is necessary.

Tied closely to the aforementioned benefit is acknowledging that change is necessary. Acknowledging a problem is important. So is, however, the need to take action. On a typical project, schedule, cost, and quality are, in fact, the most objective indicators that a problem exists on a project due to variance between planned versus actual performance. Yet, some people do not know or care about these indicators for fear of what they will reveal. Instead, they go into denial, even to the point of not implementing any disciplines associated with good project management. It's like a man with a heart problem who is in denial; he acts as if no problem exists. It's critical to acknowledge that a problem exists before determining what a solution is necessary.

Overcoming fear is another benefit. Suffice it to say that when a new project manager is selected to replace the existing one, people may become fearful of being held responsible for the state of the project. Finger-pointing and sabotage can occur.

Fear in the workplace is bad enough, but fear on a project can have just as harmful effects. Communications can stop, poor coordination can occur, non-value-added behavior can occur, and esprit de corps can decline, all coalescing to cause major schedule slippages, cost overruns, and poor quality of output. All this can increase in magnitude on top of an already poor performance record.

The best way to overcome this fear is to help people obtain a better understanding of the circumstances confronting their projects. This benefit is realized when people are energized by a new project manager. Being energized, however, is not the sole responsibility of the project manager. The stakeholders, especially the core team members, must energize themselves to make change happen, too. The best way for them to energize is, with the help of the project manager, to obtain a solid understanding of the project's state and how it should proceed from this point onward.

The ability to energize does pose some challenges that you need to recognize.

First, a project manager is an outsider and likely to be greeted in the same way that Sidney Poiter was in the classic movie, *Guess Who's Coming to Dinner?* Or worse, you could be greeted like the character in the television show *Paladin*, with everyone treating you like the expert but not wanting you present because you're the one who has to clean things up.

In other words, the chances of your coming in and making everyone feel warm and fuzzy are low. True, some people will welcome change, but others will resist any change because they have a vested interest in the status quo. It is for that reason alone that you can expect resistance. The notion that you come in metaphorically on a white horse, although it does occur sometimes, is improbable; more likely, the opposite will occur.

Related to the previous challenge is the fact that the defensiveness of many stakeholders can be quite high. These people may have invested a lot of time, effort, and emotion in the project, which may not necessarily have contributed to furthering the original vision. You have to penetrate these walls of resistance to cause change to happen. Doing so enables you to take proactive, prescriptive approaches to turn around a project. You need their cooperation to succeed. It is imperative that you overcome this challenge without having to replace the entire team (though that may be a viable option) or some or all of its members.

Low morale and poor esprit de corps probably exist, and, oddly enough, some people may be reluctant to change and cooperate. Chances are that finger-pointing will occur and communications will be abysmal. Depending on the size of the project team, a team itself will be composed of cliques and likely possess a siege mentality toward management in general and the customer in particular. Even if these conditions do not exist, you will still face quite a challenge energizing the team.

When you take over a project in trouble, expect one of two outcomes: either the core team will accept you with open arms or they will reject you outright. While the former is the ideal state, the latter is more likely. Expect resistance, and deal with it.

As you might suspect, the degree of power you have and how you apply it will have a big impact on how much cooperation or resistance you can expect to face.

According to John French and Bertram Raven, five types of power exist. These are:

- Coercive power
- Reward power
- Legitimate power
- Expert power
- Referent power

Coercive power. This type of power is based on the use of coercion or fear. Many project managers lack this power, at least overtly. Still, a project manager has the coercive power to remove people from key tasks and reassign them to someone else; inform a team member's manager about an individual's poor performance; and not invite the person to any of the team's meetings.

Coercive power tends to get immediate results, but can have long-term negative consequences. It is for this reason that it should be used sparingly, but don't discount it, because it is a tool that you can use should the situation warrant it.

Reward power. Unlike coercive power, this type of power relies on the use of positive incentives when managing projects. Many project managers fail to realize some of the reward power at their disposal. These include assigning people to high-profile tasks, recommending people for awards, and sending their functional manager a complimentary e-mail.

Positive rewards tend to have a lasting effect. However, sooner or later, reward power can lose its effectiveness if exercised indiscriminately or in a way that smacks of favoritism. Still, you should prefer it as an instrument of change over coercive power.

Legitimate power. This type of power is by virtue of your position. As the project manager of a project in trouble, you can automatically expect to have some legitimate power. Like most project managers, however, expect that legitimate power to be weak and expect that some team members will try to test it simply because you are new and they may not want you there for many reasons. Still, legitimate power can prove useful initially in moving the team toward taking meaningful action. Be aware, though, that whatever legitimate authority you may have, expect the informal power structure to challenge your legitimate powers from time to time.

Expert power. If you have been selected to take over a project in trouble, chances are you were chosen for your expertise either in project management or some other subject area. Expert power is one of the longer-lasting powers simply because it is difficult to dilute its effectiveness unless, of course, you do not stay current in your field. As a project manager who has taken over a project in trouble, you were likely chosen for your expertise at this point in time, providing you with a key instrument to leverage change on your project.

Referent power. This type of power is based on a person's characteristics, such as personality or physical stature. Referent power and expert power are two of the most effective sources of power for a project manager. The danger with referent power, however, is that sometimes expectations of stakeholders become so high that sooner or later even a modest failure to meet them can result in problems for you. You may lose credibility, thereby weakening this power.

When taking over a project in trouble, determine what power is potentially at your disposal. You will likely have multiple sources of power that you can draw upon under different circumstances. At the same time, you should identify the limitations of that power in the context you choose to exercise in it. Finally, expect consequences when you exercise power, particularly coercive power. For every action there is a corresponding reaction, according to one of Newton's laws. Expect and prepare for it.

It is important for you to have a good understanding of how energizing works. With such an understanding, you will have an easier time wrestling with the details.

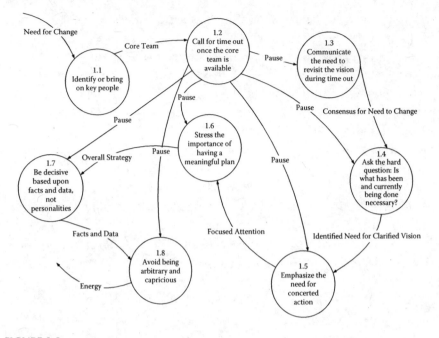

FIGURE 2.2
Level Two: Energize.

As mentioned earlier, energizing is one of the five key actions to turn a project in trouble around. It is the only one that feeds the other four key actions and is a prerequisite for meaningful change to occur.

Note in Figure 2.1 that the Action 1.0 Energize has a pound sign; this symbol indicates that the action is decomposed or exploded into finer details called activities. These activities are ones that you must perform at a minimum if you expect to get people on your project to change.

Figure 2.2 shows details of what those activities are and how they relate to each other. They are

1.1 Identify or bring on the key people.
1.2 Call for a time-out once the core team is available.
1.3 Communicate the need to revisit the vision during the time-out.
1.4 Ask the hard question: Is what has been done and is currently being done necessary?
1.5 Emphasize the need for concerted action.
1.6 Stress the importance of having a meaningful plan.
1.7 Be decisive based on facts and data, not personalities.
1.8 Avoid being arbitrary and capricious.

2.2 AN OVERVIEW

1.1 *Identify or bring on the key people.* This activity means identifying the key stakeholders on the project. These are the people who, for better or worse, can help a project manager acquire a solid understanding of what has occurred to date and with whom they need to work to receive buy-in in order to turn around a project in trouble. This activity is initiated by a request for change from either management or the customer or both.

1.2 *Call for a time-out once the core team is available.* The objective of this activity is to give time for people to think about what has happened and enable regrouping. In other words, it provides a respite from the past circumstances that led to the need for change. It also provides an opportunity to think about what can be done to improve future performance.

1.3 *Communicate the need for revisiting the vision during the time-out.* The project manager discusses the need to review the vision to ensure that it reflects reality. Core team members, possibly consisting of management and the customer, may agree that the vision is valid as it exists or that a new or revised one is necessary. Regardless, the output for this activity is a consensus over the need for change on the project.

1.4 *Ask the hard question: Is what has been done and is currently being done necessary?* This question assumes consensus over the need to do something different. Quite often, the answers you receive will indicate that many activities occur that do not support even the old vision for the project. It may even reveal people working on activities that have no relevance to the results that have been achieved to date. The important outcome from this activity is that it will likely demonstrate the need for a new, clarified, or revised vision for the project.

1.5 *Emphasize the need for concerted action.* Now is the time to take advantage of having reached a consensus. If the right questions are asked, you will likely find that the activities on a project were moving in different directions, with some supporting the vision, goals, and objectives of the project and others either irrelevant or ineffective. This information is useful for underscoring the point that the activities of a team need to be relevant and contribute toward achieving the desired results.

You could very likely face some resistance because egos are involved. Some people will protect their turf and likely disagree that what they do provides no value to the project. It is imperative, therefore, that you achieve consensus at this point, if for any reason other than to build allies for making change.

1.6 *Stress the importance of having a meaningful plan.* Just about everyone will agree that a plan is necessary, and that is the easy part. The challenge is getting themselves to change and accepting the portion of the plan that affects them.

You need to tread carefully down this path. If the project previously lacked a meaningful plan, the tendency is for people to prefer to act on their own, and they will likely have enjoyed that freedom despite the rework involved. A new plan will require greater control and oversight, which will not likely be embraced by everyone. At this point in time, it should suffice to stress the need to have a new plan that supports the new vision, goals, and objectives for the project. Remember, for this action, Energy, the key is to get people at a minimum to recognize the need for change to occur.

1.7 *Be decisive based on facts and data, not personalities.* It is important for you to demonstrate objectivity and independence. If you demonstrate contrary behavior in this regard, you may become embroiled in politics and lose all credibility. This will make it extremely difficult to implement changes and may result in your becoming ostracized from stakeholders whom you will need to work with to identify and implement changes that improve project performance.

1.8 *Avoid being arbitrary and capricious.* Once all the previous activities have occurred, this activity should be relatively easy as long as your ego is in check. In reality, this should occur throughout this activity and all the remaining activities.

The key to avoid being arbitrary and capricious is to weigh facts and data as well as to listen to the input of others before making a decision and taking action. In today's project environment, to act otherwise is to invite disaster.

2.3 1.1: IDENTIFY OR BRING ON THE KEY PEOPLE

The key objective is to identify the right people or other kinds of stakeholders to provide the necessary data and information to make a meaningful change on a project in trouble. As a general rule, the key people are often the 20% who produce 80% of the results, good and bad. These people, known as key stakeholders, have the knowledge, skills, and expertise to help identify ways to get the project back on track and direct energies into fixing high-leverage, critical problems.

The principal benefit is that it quickly enables you to build trust among customers and management alike by demonstrating a willingness to listen and work with others who already have a stake in the outcome of the project.

There is, of course, a danger that some of the 20% mentioned earlier will not welcome you and may exhibit resistance that will likely surface early through noncooperation or not sharing data, information, or ideas. You may be viewed as a threat, and their approach may be overt or subtle. The key is to snuff out this resistance as early as possible and as quickly as possible to confront issues directly and early so that they don't surface later during the recovery of the project, resulting in the same problems repeating themselves that caused the project to get in trouble in the first place.

You should, therefore, expect turning around a project in trouble to be filled with conflict. It is an inherent characteristic of such projects. You cannot avoid it, simply because you will be changing the status quo and also because it was likely handled poorly before you arrived.

Conflict of this type may be due to multiple sources, and these sources are probably no different in any other type of project except for the level of intensity, depth, breadth, and complexity. Some common sources of conflict include limited resources; management style; unrealistic schedule; ambiguous or incomplete requirements or both; complex and contradictory processes and procedures; and the ubiquitous differences in personality.

There are different ways to address conflict:

You can force a solution; however, remember that it may lack buy-in by those involved and could build resentment.

You can avoid it by ignoring it or simply pretending that it will gradually fade away. While that may happen, often the conflict resurfaces at the wrong time.

You can seek a compromise solution that achieves partial results. While that may pacify the parties involved for a while, the conflict will likely resurface as soon as some circumstance arises that aggravates the tenuous relationship.

You can make everyone feel warm and fuzzy by emphasizing mutual characteristics without having to address the conflict. Once again, however, after the cooling-off period ends, the conflict will return as soon as the source of the conflict returns.

The best approach is to face the conflict head-on and deal with it early and effectively. While this may be painful at first for yourself and the other parties, it tends to be the most effective approach. The opportunity for the conflict to later rear its head in the project subsides.

When dealing with conflict, therefore, keep in mind the following guidelines:

- Recognize that not all conflict is negative. Some conflict is healthy and positive. The positive type of conflict causes you and the members of your team to develop creative solutions to problems by challenging assumptions.
- Keep the vision in sight when resolving conflict; focus on the big picture. By keeping the vision in the forefront, you can resolve conflict based on its context, not some hidden agenda.
- Identify the source of the conflict, not its symptoms. This is a tough one. The best approach is to focus on the facts and data behind every situation requiring action. You must continuously ask "Why?" until you arrive at a satisfactory solution.
- Encourage the participants in the conflict to formulate a mutually satisfying solution rather than one imposed by you. The best solution to a conflict is the one that all parties determine to solve; otherwise, people will feel you are taking sides, and your credibility will be tarnished.
- Always follow up on the effectiveness of the solution after implementation. The reason is simple: failure to follow up will likely encourage people to ease up on its implementation, thereby diluting the effectiveness of the response.
- Address conflict as early as possible to avoid impacting the final delivery of the product. If you wait, the chances increase that the same problem will resurface with greater intensity and complexity. The longer you wait, the greater the impact on the project completion date.

2.4 1.2: CALL FOR A TIME-OUT

Whether good or bad, projects have a momentum. They are like a loco-motive hurtling down a track at 150 miles per hour, either on or off the track. Somehow or in some way, you have to force some kind of a respite to determine what has been done. Too often, especially on large projects, people find themselves working hard and doing great work, but no one is asking the fundamental question: Where are we going with all this? The project lurches onward to some destination that no one either understands or cares about. Even if they do understand or care, some people will feel that they have invested too much to determine if what they are doing is on the right track. Everyone needs to take a pause, if only a short one, if for no other reason than to think.

Calling for a time-out offers several benefits.

First, it helps to preclude a further diminution of resources. A brief hia-tus can give core team members the opportunity to think about the out-put of the project and whether it contributes toward achieving the overall vision of the project. In other words, they can think about what tasks could be halted immediately, saving time, money, and effort.

Second, it provides an opportunity to think about how the project's vision can be achieved. A temporary cessation allows people the oppor-tunity to think not only about the tasks to be done but also the vision to be achieved. Taking time to ask whether the current vision is realistic is just as important as questioning the tasks being performed. The reason is that the vision lays the groundwork for identifying the tasks to be per-formed. If the tasks are not based on the vision, then a disconnect may exist between the eventual results and the expectations of the customer, management, or both.

Third, it allows the core team to consolidate team energy. Chances are, a project in trouble is wasting the energy of its team members. Some team members are likely dissipating energy, thereby inefficiently achiev-ing results. Duplicate work and rework are two examples of energy being wasted. The key, as with other forms of energy, is to channel it produc-tively. You and your core team need to direct energies in such a way that the vision, goals, and objectives of the project are achieved.

Fourth, it gives an opportunity to determine priorities. You and your core team can determine priorities relative to the four cornerstones of

project management: cost, schedule, scope, and quality. A significant reason a project is often in trouble is because of issues related to one or more
of these four cornerstones of project management, which is why you were
invited to take over as the new project manager.

Whatever changes you make, therefore, expect to juggle four variables
to achieve the vision of the project. These four variables are cost, schedule,
quality, and scope.

All four variables are interrelated. If you make a change to cost, your
decision will affect schedule, quality, and scope. If you make a change
that affects the scope, then you will affect cost, schedule, and quality.
The same goes with the other two variables: change one, and you alter
the others.

Figure 2.3 shows this intricate relationship.

Take the following example. You select an option to reduce the scope of
your project. The impact could potentially affect the schedule by pulling
it back, reducing costs, and perhaps hindering quality. The opposite could
be the case, too. You select an option to increase the scope of your project.
The impact could potentially affect the schedule by pushing it out, increasing costs, and increasing quality standards.

Your options to improve your project will require considering the relationship among all four variables. The fundamental principle behind this
relationship is TANSTAAFL: There Ain't No Such Thing As A Free Lunch.
Although this concept has its origins in economics, it applies here, too.
Change one variable, and it will impact the others, sometimes positively,
sometimes negatively.

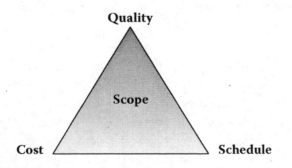

FIGURE 2.3
Project management triangle.

2.5 1.3: COMMUNICATE THE NEED FOR REVISITING THE VISION

With the core team in place and with some time available to think about current situation, the moment has arrived to raise concerns about the vision of the project. The key concern here is whether the vision, which includes goals, objectives, and acceptance criteria, are satisfactory or whether it needs revision. You may find the original vision too broad or incomplete, thereby contributing to the current state of the project. Or, you may find that the vision needs further clarification because it remains too much of an abstraction to the stakeholders, for example, the customer.

Of course, it is too premature to try to develop or revise the vision at this point in time. You are simply raising the issue so that people think about it in the context of turning around your project.

There are two benefits to raising the issue now. The first is that it gives people a sense of meaning about the project. By getting them concerned about the vision, it begins to engender a sense of ownership about the project, thereby lessening the probable feeling like they are just cogs in a machine. They may begin to feel that they can influence the project outcome.

The second benefit is that by thinking about the vision, they also start prioritizing work. Once again, they will acquire a greater sense of ownership over both current and future results. Keep in mind that no changes are made at this point.

As a new project manager, you will likely need the help of the core team to acquire as much background about the project as quickly as possible. In addition to talking with each of the core team members, you need to review documentation that helps to put the project into perspective. This documentation may be a formal document or a slide show. Specific items to look for, for example, are how the project fits within the strategic direction of the organization. In what way does it help to clarify the vision, mission, and goals of the parent organization? Is it a strategic or operational project? Answers to these questions may be found in an earlier draft of the charter, the portfolio management plans of the organization, the business case, requirements documentation, and previous reports about the performance of the project. If sources of this information are unavailable, you will need to rely on anecdotal information.

As you strive to acquire background information about the project, you will likely discover it to be a challenging exercise.

2.6 1.4: ASK THE HARD QUESTION: IS WHAT HAS BEEN AND IS CURRENTLY BEING DONE NECESSARY?

Just because people are busy does not necessarily mean that they are efficient and effective. It could be that they may be performing tasks that do not contribute to the overall success of a project and may also be doing so wastefully. It is absolutely critical to ask this question now so that people start thinking about how they can further add, or provide, value to the project. This is especially valuable because the people who do the actual work are probably best placed to answer that question. Again, you are not asking for solutions at this point, only that they think about what they are doing currently.

There are two benefits from asking this fundamental question. First, it will help you distinguish between wants and needs. It may become apparent that the results currently being produced are not critical to the success of the project or that the tasks occurring do not address the needs of the customer.

The second benefit is that it provides the necessary focus on needs that will largely determine the priorities from a deliverables perspective. There are certain minimum criteria that deliverables must meet, if adequately defined, for a project to complete successfully.

Scope creep is a major contributor to projects getting into trouble. The inability to distinguish between needs and wants often leads to gold plating, that is, delivering more than what the customer requested. This desire can lead to obliterating cost and schedule constraints as well as delivery of a product or service that exceeds costs over its life cycle.

To avoid problems such as scope creep, you will need to collect, clarify, and capture requirements from the customer. Now is a good time to start. There is a good chance that one of the reasons why your project is in trouble is that it fails to meet requirements. What makes your task even more difficult is that you and your team are on a time crunch; furthermore, the customer probably doesn't want to expend additional time that was wasted previously, resulting in the current situation.

Collecting, clarifying, and capturing requirements is not easy; you, like your predecessor, will face some serious challenges.

First, trying to persuade the customer to make the time and effort to define requirements is a challenge. The customer who views it will have other priorities, but will nevertheless expect you to make them your number-one priority.

Second, getting the customer to define what constitutes value can be difficult. Perhaps due to internal bickering or a feeling that everything is important, the customer just might assume that every requirement is equally important. Of course, not all requirements are equal; some are more important than others, but from a customer satisfaction perspective, you and your team should avoid making that call. The customer should make the decision.

Third, having the customer set priorities is a challenge. Obviously, if the customer has a problem defining value, then part of the problem will be the customer's inability to determine priorities simply because they has no reference point from which to make that decision.

Fourth, determining who speaks for the customer is a challenge, especially with a large customer. The customer, as an organization, may not be able to speak with unanimity about requirements. This situation can result in constant churning of content and scope, causing widespread frustration.

Fifth, determining when you've captured all the requirements necessary to turn around the project is yet another challenge. That's one of the biggest challenges in requirements: ascertaining how much is enough. The danger of not being able to determine when you're done is that the project can fall into analysis paralysis, causing one delay after another in the recovery and adding to costs.

Sixth, another challenge is determining the solution to the requirements prior to having them defined up front. Under pressure to recover a failing project, a project manager may determine a solution first and then later go back and capture requirements. While this approach may obtain quick results in the short term, it may do harm in the long term. Consequently, the solution may not fit the needs or wants of the customer, leading to dissatisfaction once again.

Seventh, determining the most appropriate tool or model for capturing requirements can become a challenge. You need to select a tool or modeling technique that everyone understands, yet provides you and your team with the necessary information to satisfy the customer. Too complex a tool or model will turn them off; too simple a tool or model, and the feedback could be dismissed as useless and a waste of time.

Eighth, ascertaining the best way to elicit requirements can pose a significant challenge. Do you and your team have a group meeting? Do you hold meetings in one-on-one sessions? Do you work with liaisons or customer representatives? Each approach has its positives and negatives, usually involving a trade-off among time, cost, and quality.

Finally, determining how to go about validating requirements can pose a challenge. You and your team will face issues of ambiguity around terminology, completeness, complexity, stability, and traceability of requirements. How will requirements get cast in concrete? For example, how will changes to requirements be managed?

Although the challenges seem overwhelming, you and your team have more options than you think, especially since you are taking over a project in trouble.

First, when collecting requirements, set what is known as a *time box*. Because you are in recovery mode, you will need to set a time frame, likely compressed, to collect a suitable set of requirements. This will help to preclude falling into a typical endless spiral that often occurs when collecting requirements. Of course, make sure the customer agrees with the length of the time box.

Second, consider building a prototype to represent the requirements. The prototype is a model of what the customer needs, and it can be a paper or electronic model. A prototype provides immediate feedback on whether the requirements are sufficient and accurate. Of course, developing a prototype depends on whether the project can accommodate such an approach.

Third, place requirements under change management once they have been captured. After capturing a new or revised set of requirements, do not allow any modifications unless they have been formally approved by both parties. This will prevent the all-too-common phenomenon of scope creep, which hurts many projects. A series of minor changes can result cumulatively in a large change that can cause a project to spiral out of control. You need to set a baseline for the set of requirements for the project; otherwise, you will be shooting at a moving target.

2.7 1.5: EMPHASIZE THE NEED FOR CONCERTED ACTION

Hopefully, the core team members have by now reached a consensus over the need to revisit the vision; reviewing past and current work, and eliminating non-value-added tasks. With a consensus in place, the team is now mentally prepared to turn around your project.

Concentrating on improving or replanning is critical. Too often, project teams dissipate their energies, exerting considerable effort but achieving little in return toward realizing the vision, goals, and objectives of a project. This situation may occur owing to poor managerial oversight, inadequate quality of technical work, or an attempt to satisfy too many priorities set by higher management. Regardless of the reason, consensus is necessary to move forward to the next major action, Envision; otherwise, overt and subtle resistance will likely occur and may make identifying, developing, and implementing substantive changes challenging at best. Little or no consensus, of course, does not necessarily mean the project cannot move forward; it simply means that the project manager and certain core team members will likely experience greater frustration in their endeavors to improve project performance.

Naturally, as a new project manager you would like everyone on the team, especially core team members, to agree wholeheartedly with the vision, new plans, and other changes. Agreement, of course, means that nothing can proceed until everyone accepts everything as it stands. No disagreement is allowed.

Of course, such a requirement would make it impossible for the project to move forward. One hundred percent agreement over everything is next to impossible to attain, nor is it worthwhile. To think otherwise would stall progress, bog it down into debate over meaningless detail, and probably add to the existing negative conflict.

What you want to attain is consensus over the major deliverables. With a consensus, people can disagree over some details and yet support any change, decision, or action.

The key to achieving consensus is to get people to understand the essence of any change, decision, or action you take. Then, seek their acceptance of at least the spirit behind the change, decision, or action. Finally, once you gain their acceptance, ask for their support.

Consensus is an excellent way to avoid delays in moving forward. It eliminates the possibility that one individual can filibuster or negate the desire of others to move forward. It keeps people focused on the overall need to turn around the project in many different ways. Again, under a consensus, team members seek to understand first, then give their general consent from a larger perspective and provide support.

Even when consensus is difficult to attain, you should focus your discussions on the overall vision and away from the details; fewer people question the intent behind something than insignificant details because the former is more abstract. This approach can help circumvent arguments over minutia.

Upon reaching a consensus, advertise having attained it. This approach will make people reluctant to express disapproval. After all, giving consent and making it public makes it very difficult to backtrack without having to say "I made a mistake."

Once you take over a project in trouble, you will likely have a team that needs rejuvenation when it comes to motivation. Morale and esprit de corps will probably be low due to the negative experiences of the past.

You should be aware that the indicators of low morale and poor esprit de corps on a project are innumerable. Below, however, is a list of some common ones that you should be aware of when taking over a project in trouble.

Prevalence of fear. Team members keep to themselves or stop communicating because they expect blatant or indirect retaliation from peers, the project manager, or functional management. If fear prevails, take action to reduce it. Some ways to reduce fear are to conduct more one-on-one sessions, share more information about the status of the project, and encourage more participative decision making.

Burnout. Too much overtime due to unrealistic timelines, ill-defined requirements, or impractical workloads can burn out even the most skillful, talented team member. If this has occurred substantially in the past, you should address it. Some ways to reduce burnout include a more equitable sharing of the workload, conducting more frequent off-sites, restricting the levels of overtime, and creating a schedule based on realistic time and scope parameters.

Turnover. The constant arrival and departure of team members, especially in the early and middle phases of a project, is a good barometer on issues—especially hidden ones—impacting progress. Turnover is a sign that people are unhappy, and as the new project manager you should try to determine the reasons for its existence and take action to reverse the trend. Some actions to reduce turnover include encouraging investment in the outcome of the project by encouraging participation in the planning and management of the project and giving greater visibility to team member contributions.

Absenteeism. As with turnover, a high rate of absenteeism may reflect an underlying people problem. People calling in sick or taking days without pay may reflect an underlying or overt unhappiness about the project. Try to uncover the reasons for high absenteeism. Some ways to reduce absenteeism are to provide cross-training, allow for greater involvement in planning, and encourage more responsibility over output.

Apathy. Sometimes, when the performance of a project deteriorates, apathy starts to infect the team. This apathy, reflected in procrastination and a "don't-care" attitude, causes a project to slide further. To counter apathy, try to involve team members when developing the vision and planning and assign greater responsibility for completing discrete units of work, such as deliverables.

Lack of trust and credibility. Closely allied with the prevalence of fear, this indicator results from a lack of credibility with team members or leadership or both. Lack of trust has severe consequences, because people cannot or will not rely on decisions or communications from fellow team members or leaders up the chain of command. People will not share thoughts or information, will not work comfortably with or rely on others, thereby taking an "I'll do it myself" attitude. Some ways to restore trust and credibility include communicating frequently and honestly; encouraging leaders, including the project manager, to "walk the talk"; and allowing team members to engage in the decision-making process. As the new project manager, you will have to work the hardest to establish trust because some team members will see you as a representative of the functional leadership and in all likelihood do not know you.

Negative conflict. As emphasized in other sections of this book, not all conflict is negative; people can disagree and still work with one another. However, from time to time, the conflict can turn negative, and the tension at a meeting feels like an impenetrable wall. No one listens. Conversation is muted and, if it happens, resembles a minefield. No sense of humor or fun exists. The body language tells the entire story without anyone uttering a word. The environment is downright nasty. Often, a project manager taking over a project in trouble faces this situation. If you are one of those unlucky project managers, here are some actions you can take: build plans that encourage greater interdependence among team members, address conflict early on rather than let it fester, have more team celebrations, and have team members take psychological or team building training.

Cliques. It is human nature for groups of people to "coalesce" into cliques, that is, into groups of people who share common beliefs, values, interests, etc. Occasionally, however, a clique can become so powerful that it becomes uncontrollable, almost to the point of sidelining not just the new project manager but also functional management. Cliques can have deleterious effects. Some ways to deal with cliques are to encourage greater sharing of responsibilities among team members; give greater visibility to the people outside the dominant clique; seek alternative sources of help on the project, such as contractors; enlarge the membership of your core team; and, if necessary, remove members of the clique who fail to cooperate.

In all likelihood, your taking over a project in trouble will arouse one or more of the following emotional states in stakeholders: frustration, fear, or negativity. Expect motivational hurdles to overcome. The challenge is to motivate the key stakeholders, which includes the project team, on an individual and team level.

From an individual perspective, you need to be familiar with the work of motivational theorists, such as David McClelland on the need for power, achievement, and love; Douglas McGregor on positive and negative perspectives on people; Abraham Maslow on hierarchy of needs; and Frederick Herzberg on satisfiers and dissatisfiers, to name just a few.

The point is that people are motivated for different reasons. You need to uncover those reasons so that you can synchronize the work to be done in a way that meets the goals and objectives of the project and still, to the extent possible, satisfies the needs of the individual. Here are some ways to accomplish this:

- Be honest; do not sacrifice credibility. If you do, expect your job as a project manager to get harder, not easier.
- Confront negative behavior right away, such as complacency, carelessness, resignation, or anger. If you don't, it will resurface at the worst time, such as the time for handing over the final deliverable to the customer.
- Consider different perspectives by enhancing diversity of thought; it is unrealistic to expect people to see things exactly as you do.

- Empower people. By doing so, you increase ownership and commitment.
- Keep one-on-one sessions confidential; failure to do so will hurt your credibility and trust.
- Meet with key stakeholders individually from time to time. This will enable you to maintain an ongoing dialogue with them.
- Seek win-win, not win-lose, relationships; otherwise, expect a pay-back and lack of commitment.
- Share information. By doing so, you encourage trust among stake-holders and reduce surprises.

You will not only have to look at motivation from an individual perspective but also from a group perspective. From a team perspective, you will need to look for opportunities to improve synergy. You will first, though, have to look for indicators of dysfunction. These include

- Focus on the process rather than end results. A common vision will help you to counter this dysfunction because the focus becomes "what" and not "how."
- Groupthink (extreme conformity, causing intolerance and developing an unrealistic appraisal of situations). This can squash new ideas.
- High turnover and absenteeism. This circumstance can cause a brain drain as well as burning out the remaining team members, who assume additional workloads.
- Low or no esprit de corps. This can lead to rework and lack of commitment to the project's vision.
- Negative conflict, including political infighting; it can resurface at the wrong time during a project's life cycle.
- No clarity of roles and responsibilities, for example, roles, accountability, and authority. This situation can lead to power struggles and lack of teaming.
- No commitment to achieving the overall vision of the project. The emotional involvement by stakeholders is gone, and everyone is it for themselves.
- No sharing of resources, including data and information. This can lead to miscommunications.
- Not focusing on priorities; team members become reactive to circumstances.

The Tuchman Model, developed by Bruce Tuchman, describes the four phases that a project goes through and is an excellent tool to assess the health of a team. In recent years, a fifth phase has been added, which is covered below.

Forming phase. In this phase, the team forms. It has all the characteristics of a new team. People are getting to know each other and the basic information about the project.

Storming phase. Team members start working out the details of the project, for example, general roles and responsibilities, decision-making authority. Often, the initial good feelings vanish as people start testing each other in terms of power and position.

Norming phase. The norming phase is when most or all the differences and serious disputes have been settled, and the team is prepared to move forward. Team members and other key stakeholders are ready to cooperate. A rhythm arises that drives performance.

Performing phase. In this phase, team members focus on the vision, goals, and objectives; everyone knows and meets expectations about themselves and others; and they are receptive to new ideas.

Adjourning phase. After achieving the vision, goals, and objectives of a project, the team and other stakeholders celebrate.

When a project finds itself in trouble, it is likely the team has not resolved many issues that have arisen during the forming and storming phases. Some of these issues concern the lack of consensus around the vision, goals, objectives, and plans for the project. Other issues concern the lack of effective people skills among the participants, lack of support from management, and little or no team building. Whatever the reason, you will have to tackle the causes up front and make substantive changes that will enable your team to progress past the storming phase and into the norming and performing ones. The five actions described in this book will enable you to do just that.

Before you turn around your troubled project from the perspective of the Tuchman model, consider the following. Most teams go through this cycle, but many projects in trouble never resolve some of the issues in the forming and storming phases. If they do get to the performing and norming phases, there is a good chance that the ignored issues will surface at the wrong time. Also, recognize that different projects progress through each of the phases at different speeds. Expect obstacles and challenges in each phase; nothing works perfectly. Try leveraging the positive aspects, and deal directly with the negative ones. Finally, a project in trouble often finds its roots in the unresolved issues in the forming and storming phases that when left unattended to can complicate and threaten performance during the norming and performing phases.

Teaming just doesn't happen by itself; left without the project manager's guidance, a team, like any system, can move into disequilibrium, producing poor results. The likelihood of a project producing good results with poor teaming is remote, and the likelihood of producing good results with solid teaming is great. So, the question is, how do you encourage good teaming, especially on a project that is in trouble?

One, ensure that effective, ongoing communications is occurring. You can accomplish that by developing a communications plan that encourages greater sharing of information, dialogue, and feedback.

Two, assign roles, responsibilities, and authorities clearly. You can do that by producing an organization chart and creating a responsibility assignment matrix.

Three, apply the concept of span of control. If you need to institute leads, avoid having more than nine people reporting to each one.

Four, follow the concept of unity of command. Avoid having team members support more than one lead from a formal reporting standpoint; otherwise, these team members may find themselves crosswise with each lead.

Five, build trust among team members. You can assign team members to tasks that require more than one person.

Six, have everyone, even during times of conflict and stress, focus on the vision for the project. When conflict or problems arise, you should frame solutions according to the perspective of the vision. This approach appeals to mutual, rather than individual, interests.

Seven, provide for a positive atmosphere. You should emphasize the need for tolerance of different ideas when tackling problems or challenges by embracing diversity of thought as well as of race, religion, etc.; celebrate major achievements; and encourage cross-training.

Eight, identify and apply ground rules for the team to work together. Ideally, have the team set their own rules, but if they can't, then identify them yourself. The rules should also include ways to manage conflict, especially conflict of the negative type.

Nine, remove obstacles to performance. Often, these obstacles are an unrealistic schedule, limited resources, unclear standards of performance, poor delineation of responsibilities, and bureaucracy. You should seek to address these areas through improvements. Not tackling them will only hinder teaming.

Finally, encourage a sense of commitment on the part of the individual team members and the team as a whole. You can do that by involving people in producing project deliverables, including a new or revised work breakdown structure, schedule, estimates, and other pertinent project deliverables. You can have most or all of the team members participate in creating them.

You may find yourself dealing with one circumstance that can prove troubling as you try to build an effective team. Some people by their very nature do not like to team. Assuming they are not mavericks, these people just enjoy working alone. Nothing is wrong with that as long as the tasks require working alone; however, all tasks are not like that on a project. So, how do you get a nonteamer to team?

One way is to hold meetings that require nonteamers to attend and then take attendance. Obviously, the nonteamer will likely not attend. You then take one step further: publish the attendance record of the meeting, sending a copy to him or her. Sooner or later, a trend will surface and, if the person is smart, he or she will start attending project meetings.

Another method is to assign a nonteamer tasks that require reporting back to the rest of the team at specific meetings held in the future. This approach should entice him or her to be present at meetings, and hopefully engage in a constructive dialogue with the rest of the team.

Still another approach is to assign tasks that by their very nature require working with other people to produce a result. The outcome, in other words, necessitates collaborating with others to complete the work. Hopefully, it will prove to be a good lesson in cooperation and communication for everyone and not just for the nonteamer.

A negative approach is that if a nonteamer continues to refuse to team, you can show everyone how each person's work contributes to the others and then illustrate how a nonteamer's failure to team affects other individuals' and the entire project's performance. Just the mere discussion will point a finger at the nonteamer without specifically naming him or her.

If a nonteamer refuses to cooperate, then the best course of action is to remove that person from the project. Failure to do so will not only lower morale and esprit de corps but also cause a decline in overall project performance.

Project management by its very nature is a teaming endeavor, requiring a producer and customer at the very minimum. The inability to work as a team player can quickly degrade individual and project performance.

2.8 1.6: STRESS THE IMPORTANCE OF HAVING A MEANINGFUL PLAN

Assuming you have a consensus, you can now stress the need to have a meaningful plan. In theory, if the vision, goals, and objectives of the project change, then so should the corresponding plans. Failure to link the two can result in something akin to a layered cake gone askew, with the top layer out of alignment with the bottom one.

Many explanations exist for what contributes to making a plan unrealistic. Poor costs, schedule, and quality performance are the major contributors. An unrealistic plan exhibits one or more of these three characteristics: resources are misallocated, important milestone dates are missed, and output is riddled with defects. If in trouble, a project is likely to exhibit these symptoms, thereby requiring a more meaningful plan.

A new or revised plan offers two major benefits. First, it provides people with a sense of direction by offering a road map to achieving the vision, goals, and objectives for a project. Metaphorically, the vision is a mountaintop, and the schedule represents the route for scaling the peak. Second, a new or revised plan should instill greater confidence in achieving the vision, goals, and objectives. Without that plan, the current circumstances could likely recur, resulting in the project getting into trouble again. Once you do not develop the plan at this point in time, you achieve consensus that a new one is necessary.

2.9 1.7: BE DECISIVE BASED ON FACTS AND DATA, NOT PERSONALITIES

Although this activity is discussed now, in truth you should perform it throughout the project. Your credibility is now on the line. It is absolutely critical, therefore, that you not embroil yourself in the negative politics that likely contributed to the dire circumstances of your project in the first place. It is hard enough for a new project manager to come aboard and exert formal and informal power to institute the necessary changes. It is important to recognize that some stakeholders will not relish the idea of having a new project manager. It is imperative, therefore, that you stick to the facts and data, and not get embroiled in a situation that requires posturing based on personalities.

A project in trouble is likely to include people with a fair amount of emotional baggage. This baggage can entrap you. The best approach is to emphasize that the past no longer matters, only the future; and it is the future that should be the major concern. You should also emphasize once again that people should concentrate on facts and data coupled with decisive, focused action to turn around the project.

One benefit of this activity is that it demonstrates the project manager's desire and need to objectively manage the project. In addition, it helps build credibility with stakeholders, especially with team members. In other words, it builds trust, which increases the likelihood that people will be willing to share information with the project managers, which in turn will provide opportunities to improve project performance.

2.10 1.8: AVOID BEING ARBITRARY AND CAPRICIOUS

Sometimes, when a new project manager comes on board, he or she feels the need to "kick ass and take no prisoners." He or she fails to listen to the advice of others and will not negotiate or even hold a civil discussion. The temptation is to become heroic, someone who arrives on a white horse to save the day. While sometimes this approach works, more often than not it backfires. You should avoid it.

The last thing you should do is act in an arbitrary and capricious fashion, thereby putting everyone and the project once again at risk. An attempt to make an example of someone often just does not work because it generates fear, which in turn causes the sharing of data and information to cease or become "slanted," thereby lessening the opportunity for objective and independent discussion and decision making. It also communicates a message to others that their previous work had little or no value. The seeds for power struggles will then be planted, either now or later.

You should come aboard with a positive "can-do" attitude that conveys a sincere desire to work with the team. You can exhibit this attitude by collecting facts and data; consulting with others (initially with the core team and then with the others, if possible); and maintaining your objectivity and independence.

This approach offers two benefits. First, you lay the groundwork for encouraging ownership and commitment on the part of team members. Second, and perhaps more importantly, the team's perspective of you shifts from your project to "our" project. Their entire perception of the project shifts to something external to one intertwined with their own interests.

To successfully turn around a project in trouble, you will not only need to manage the project, you will need to lead it.

Managing the project pertains to the science of project management. It involves applying the concepts and principles of project management as well as its tools and techniques. It is about "doing things right." While it is no easy task in itself, neither is the other part, that is, leading.

Leading is about motivating people to move forward, to embrace change, and to give that "extra" which differentiates itself from the routine or normal way. It involves the soft side, or art, of project management. As a project manager, when leading, you do a lot of communicating, conflict resolution, negotiating, active listening, and encouraging people to be creative and take ownership of their role.

Here are some ways to demonstrate that you are not being arbitrary and capricious.

One, ask for insights on new ways to address persistent problems on the project. By asking this question, you will discover the individuals who truly have an interest in the outcome of the project. People who do not respond or come up with the same old ideas are likely not candidates to assume greater responsibilities on the project.

Two, ask for volunteers to take on greater responsibilities. Natural leaders among the team will want to contribute more. They will look for ways even if you don't ask for volunteers. By asking, you get a good idea who they are.

Three, look for people who are willing to accept responsibility for something that went wrong and who can accept responsibility for what happened. They do not blame others for tasks that they performed poorly. They don't whine. They learn from their failures and make an effort in good faith to improve their performance in the future even if it isn't perfect once again.

Four, seek out people who act without waiting to be told what to do. In other words, they initiate, not procrastinate. They are proactive, meaning they do not wait for something to come to them or for it to happen; they anticipate and expend the energy in advance.

To encourage such leadership, you can take several actions as the project leader.

One, you can reward leadership. Rewards may take the form of a special recognition award at a fancy restaurant or a simple thank-you by senior management or yourself.

Two, allude to individuals who exhibit leadership at meetings. Do it in a way, of course, that does not embarrass the individuals or encourage behind-the-back sneers or attacks by people who did not exhibit leadership.

Three, encourage participation in decision making. Through participation, you not only get commitment but you often find people wanting to participate in its execution. Your management style, however, must be conducive to this type of approach. Otherwise, people will view your efforts as not being genuine.

You need to be attuned to the sources of shortcomings. You should also be mindful of the many symptoms of poor leadership that may be exhibited by key stakeholders in general and the previous project manager in particular. These symptoms and their consequences are

- Blaming or scapegoating: No one takes responsibility for results.
- Dishonesty: Credibility and trust are sacrificed.
- Emphasis on quantity over quality: Rework becomes the norm.
- Firefighting: Reactive management becomes a way of life.
- Ineffective and unmanageable meetings: A waste of time and other resources that jeopardize productivity.
- Inflexibility: Good ideas fall by the wayside.
- Lack of empathy: Negative conflict becomes commonplace.
- Low acceptance of risk: This results in lost opportunities to improve performance.
- Low morale: This contributes to poor individual performance.
- Micromanaging: This causes a lack of trust and commitment.
- Misallocation of resources: This leads to excessive consumption of labor and nonlabor assets.
- No accountability or responsibility: No one assumes responsibility for results.
- Not delegating: This causes a lack of trust.
- Poor communications: People find themselves wasting their time and energy.
- Poor planning: This results in poor performance.
- Task oriented, not results oriented: Quality is sacrificed.
- Unclear goals and objectives: This leads to reactive behavior.

The list can go on, of course, but building an exhaustive list is not the point. The key point is that you need to give leadership as much care and attention to managing; in fact, a good case can be made for a greater emphasis on leading.

You are uniquely positioned to work with a wide array of stakeholders. You are the only one who interfaces with all of them, acting as a hub. Leading is instrumental in getting everyone to participate and, just as importantly, continuing to participate throughout the life cycle of the project.

Essentially, leadership behavior should be more transformational than transactional in orientation. You seek to maintain what is positive from the past but endeavor to take the project to a higher level of productivity in the future. You will likely require taking a more assertive approach toward achieving that new performance level.

Note the choice of words: assertive, not aggressive. Assertive is taking a positive approach toward achieving the goals and objectives of the project, relying more on persuasion, communicating, negotiating, etc., which leads to win-win results. Aggressiveness relies more on threats and other negative incentives, resulting in a win-lose outcome. Contemporary thinking on leadership stresses the need to be assertive.

The key to exhibiting assertive behavior is applying an appropriate leadership style to energize the team throughout the life cycle of the project. The three predominant styles are applying the trait, situational, and behavioral leadership styles. Trait theory, which forces on the physical qualities of an individual, no longer has much creditability, though it can still influence the outcome of a project. Situational leadership involves adapting one's approach to leadership depending on the circumstances. Behavioral leadership involves motivating people by addressing psychological and sociological factors. Contemporary thinking favors the situational and behavioral styles. The key is for you to select the style that works best for you, which is often a hybrid of the two main theories.

2.11 CONCLUSION

Energizing—that is, providing the "spark" for making change happen—is vitally important for turning around a project in trouble. Failure to provide that spark can mean that the situation will not change, or perhaps it may deteriorate. As a project manager, you are the one person who can provide that spark, because you are not only responsible for the outcome of a project but also because you interact with just about all the key stakeholders. By adding that spark, the fire for change can come from within and spread among all the stakeholders, invigorating them all toward constructive action leading to success.

Case Study (*Continued*)

Energize. Deborah, at a staff meeting, was introduced to the organization as the new project manager for the LIBI application. While management had endorsed Deborah, it was not the same for some of the team members. The team was split in half over the change; some were loyal to Harold and felt that they had something to lose from the transition; the other half was neutral at best with a few exceptions. Deborah was perceived to be a representative from management. Harold made it quite known that he was displeased with his not remaining both the project manager and the system architect. The tension that was already negative between Harold and several members of the team, along with Fred, had intensified.

Immediately, Deborah had meetings with Fred, and her manager, and management from the internal customer. She wanted to understand the issues from a strategic level so that she received a good understanding of the context. Then, with Fred's help, she wanted to determine the core team members on the project. She asked whether the vision for the project was adequate, if current output was relevant, and other facts and data necessary for improving the project.

Armed with this knowledge, Deborah held a team meeting with the core team members to understand the issues, challenges, problems, and opportunities concerning the project. As expected, Harold and a few of the core team members boycotted the meeting; however, the vast majority of the core team attended. As with management and the internal customer, she asked whether the vision for the project was adequate, if current output was relevant, and other facts and data necessary for improving the project.

She then held meetings with each of the core team members to understand their issues, challenges, and problems. She stressed in each of these sessions that everything would be kept confidential but did mention that the results would be compiled in a manner that did not reveal the source.

Harold was not pleased. He expressed concern that individual sessions were a waste of time, that developers had more important concerns like writing code. He declined to meet with Deborah.

After completing all the interviews, Deborah held a team meeting and showed a compilation of the results to get feedback. After some discussion, Deborah obtained consensus over the results. Again, Harold decided not to attend. However, everyone else on the core team decided to do so. It was abundantly clear that the project lacked focus and that a considerable amount of activity was not achieving much of the current vision for the project. She then asked for consensus over not just the results but also a need to revisit the vision and develop a more useful plan. Everyone expressed consensus, including Fred. Deborah was very conscious of not proceeding in an arbitrary or capricious manner, unlike the previous project manager.

Based on management's and the core team's feedback, Deborah then needed time with the core team to develop a new vision and approach to the project. After a few discussions with Fred, she was granted three days to understand the current vision and develop a new one for the project and come up with a new game plan for turning around the project. The meeting was conducted at an off-site location so that people were not distracted.

2.11 GETTING-STARTED CHECKLIST

Question	Yes	No
1. When talking with team members, do you gain consensus over:		
Acceptance that the past has not worked?	___	___
A need for change exists?	___	___
The need to control their destiny?	___	___
Their need to overcome fear?	___	___
An understanding of their circumstances?	___	___
2. Have you considered how to address the following challenges that you will face in Energizing the team:		
Being viewed as an outsider?	___	___

Question	Yes	No
The defensiveness of some of the stakeholders?	___	___
Low morale and esprit de corps?	___	___
3. Will you identify the key stakeholders?	___	___
4. When dealing with conflict, do you		
Recognize that not all conflict is negative?	___	___
Keep the vision in sight?	___	___
Identify the source of the conflict, not the symptoms?	___	___
Encourage stakeholders in the conflict to formulate a mutually satisfactory solution?	___	___
Follow up on the effectiveness of a solution?	___	___
Address the conflict as early as possible?	___	___
5. Are you thinking about calling for a time-out?	___	___
If so, will you use it as an opportunity to		
Prevent the continued diminution of resources?	___	___
Allow time to think about the overall vision of the project?	___	___
Consolidate team energy by identifying any immediate non-value-added work?	___	___
Review existing priorities?	___	___
6. Do you communicate the need to revisit the vision?	___	___
If so, will you		
Communicate a sense of meaning about the project?	___	___
Encourage thinking about the priorities of the project?	___	___
Use it as an opportunity to acquire background information about the project?	___	___
7. Did you ask the hard question: Is what has been, and is currently being done, necessary?	___	___
If so, did you discuss some of the following items as possible contributors to scope creep?	___	___
Lack of time and effort to define requirements	___	___
Defining what constitutes value	___	___
Setting priorities	___	___
Determining who speaks for the customer	___	___
Determining when or whether all requirements have been captured	___	___
Defining the problem before determining the solution	___	___
Choosing the most appropriate tool or model for capturing requirements	___	___
Validating requirements	___	___
8. When discussing requirements, do you consider the following options?		
Time boxing	___	___
Prototyping or modeling	___	___
Change management	___	___

Question	Yes	No
9. Will you emphasize the need for concerted action?	____	____
10. Do you look for indicators of poor morale and esprit de corps, like		
Prevalence of fear?	____	____
Burnout?	____	____
Turnover?	____	____
Absenteeism?	____	____
Apathy?	____	____
Lack of trust or credibility?	____	____
Negative conflict?	____	____
Presence of cliques?	____	____
11. Do you consider the following techniques for uncovering obstacles to motivation?		
Meeting with key stakeholders individually	____	____
Empowering people	____	____
Seeking win-win relationships	____	____
Enhancing diversity of thought	____	____
Being honest	____	____
Keeping one-on-one sessions confidential	____	____
Sharing of information	____	____
Confronting negative behavior right away	____	____
12. Do you look for any indicators of dysfunctional team behavior, like		
Groupthink?	____	____
No clarity on roles and responsibilities?	____	____
Low or no esprit de corps?	____	____
Negative conflict?	____	____
No commitment to achieving the overall vision?	____	____
Focusing on process rather than end results?	____	____
High turnover and absenteeism?	____	____
No sharing of information and other resources?	____	____
Not focusing on priorities?	____	____
13. Do you determine whether, using the Tuchman model, the team is in the following phase:		
Forming?	____	____
Storming?	____	____
Norming?	____	____
Performing?	____	____
Adjourning?	____	____
14. To improve teaming, do you		
Ensure that effective ongoing communications is occurring?	____	____
Define roles, responsibilities, and authorities clearly?	____	____

Question	Yes	No
Apply the concept of span of control?	____	____
Apply the concept of unity of command?	____	____
Build trust among team members?	____	____
Focus on the vision?	____	____
Encourage diversity of thinking?	____	____
Apply conflict resolution and negotiating skills?	____	____
Adopt an organizational structure conducive to the norms of the team?	____	____
Facilitate relationships among team members through interaction, integration, and interdependence?	____	____
Articulate policies, processes, and procedures?	____	____
Celebrate the completion of major milestones?	____	____
15. Do you stress the importance of having a meaningful plan?	____	____
16. Are you being decisive based on facts and data, not personalities?	____	____
17. Are you avoiding being arbitrary and capricious by		
Exhibiting a positive attitude?	____	____
Leading as well as managing?	____	____
18. Are you aware of the following symptoms of poor leadership?		
Dishonesty	____	____
Not delegating	____	____
Micromanaging	____	____
Unclear goals and objectives	____	____
Poor communications	____	____
Ineffective and unmanageable meetings	____	____
Risk aversion	____	____
Lack of empathy	____	____
Blaming or scapegoating	____	____
Firefighting	____	____
Inflexibility	____	____
Task oriented as opposed to result oriented?	____	____
Emphasis on quantity over quality	____	____
Misallocation of resources	____	____
Tolerance for low morale	____	____
No accountability or responsibility	____	____
Poor planning	____	____
19. Do you seek to encourage the leadership capabilities of team members by		
Asking for insights on new ways to address persistent problems on a project?	____	____
Asking for volunteers to take on greater responsibilities?	____	____

Question	Yes	No
Look for people willing to accept responsibility for something that went wrong?	____	____
Seek people who take action without being told what to do?	____	____
Encourage participation in discussions and decision making?	____	____
20. If you have one or more people who do not like to team, did you consider		
Holding team meetings, and taking and publishing attendance?	____	____
Assigning the nonteamer with activities that require reporting back to the team at a specific meeting in the future?	____	____
Assigning the nonteamer to activities that require working with other people to produce a deliverable?	____	____
Show to everyone how each person's work contributes to the others' work and then illustrate how nonteaming affects individual and overall performance?	____	____
Request that the person be removed from the project?	____	____

3

Envision

3.1 AN OVERVIEW

With the spark having ignited the stakeholders, including core team members, the next action to take is Envision (Figure 3.1), that is, revisiting the vision and developing a new or revised vision.

If your project is in trouble, it is very likely that the cause is a problem with the vision. Why? It may be that the vision is too complex for anyone to understand. It may be that the vision is too broad to have any meaning. It may be that the vision is unachievable in the context. It may mean that the vision was inappropriate from the start or has no key stakeholder support. Whatever the reason, you need to understand the existing vision first and then make the necessary changes with the participation of key stakeholders, including core team members.

The vision consists of the project charter, statement of work, requirements, specifications, and other artifacts. It is critical for one simple reason. It serves as a basis for setting expectations, constructing plans, and managing the project. It lays the groundwork for building the work breakdown structure, estimating time, assigning resources, and subsequently monitoring and executing the project. If the vision is flawed, its imperfections will radiate throughout the life cycle of the project. The project can find itself in trouble.

To ensure that the vision is useful for turning around your project, you can perform these activities (as shown in Figure 3.2):

2.1 Identify stakeholders.
2.2 Take a systems approach.
2.3 Conduct a gap analysis of what was and what should have been done.
2.4 Take a snapshot of what has been going well ... and not too well.

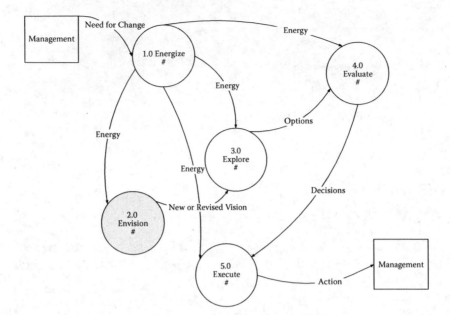

FIGURE 3.1
Level One Overview: Envision.

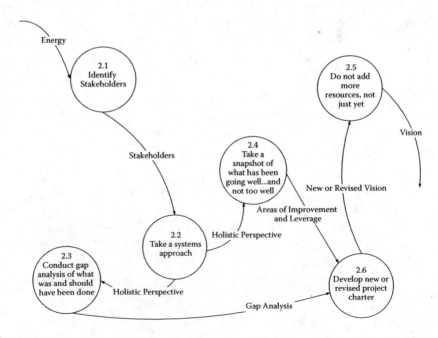

FIGURE 3.2
Level Two: Envision.

2.5 Do not add more people or functionality—not just yet.

2.6   Develop a new or revised project charter/statement of work.

2.1 *Identify stakeholders.* Once Energy has impacted the core team, a project manager can start to identify direct and indirect stakeholders. A stakeholder is someone or an organization that has an interest in your project's outcome.

Direct stakeholders have a vital interest in a project's outcome. Success or failure from a cost, schedule, or quality perspective will impact them substantially. Examples of stakeholders are individuals or organizations providing financial and other support, for example, the project sponsor or the recipient of the final product, that is, the customer.

Indirect stakeholders are people or organizations that have an interest in the outcome of the project but would not be impacted to the degree that a direct stakeholder would should the project fail. The loss or gains (if any) may be minimal should it fail or succeed, respectively. An additional example of this type of stakeholder is an individual or organization that could have leveraged the output of a project but would not suffer harm due to failure.

2.2 *Take a systems approach.* After identifying stakeholders, you along with your core team should take a systems perspective of the project. A systems perspective requires looking at the project holistically by identifying all the automated and manual processes and components along with the stakeholders and determining how everything and everyone interact to deliver the product. This knowledge will enable you and your team to understand the context and intricacies of the project.

2.3 *Conduct a gap analysis of what was and what should have been done.* The idea is to pinpoint the deficiencies of the vision, expectations, and results. Obviously, if you have come aboard on the request of the management or the customer or both, then it is safe to assume that your predecessor did not live up to at least some expectations. A systems view can provide data and information to determine whether the current problems were due to the efforts of the team. With a systems perspective, you will be able to ascertain what should have been done.

2.4 *Take a snapshot of what has been going well … and not too well.* Armed with a systemic perspective and an understanding of the gaps, you can then take a snapshot of what went well and what did not go too well. This activity emphasizes the quality of the effort and output. Certain processes and outputs may have been performed with great difficulty or performed wastefully. This analysis may reveal reasons why the project is in trouble. Coupled with a systems perspective, you and your core team should be able to ascertain what had and had not been going well from a macro and micro perspective, thereby generating ideas to improve and leverage output from previous work.

2.5 *Do not add more people or functionality—at least not yet.* This activity emphasizes not doing anything—adding more people or functionality—at least for the moment. To do otherwise may actually add to the project's problems, simply because the analysis is incomplete. A tendency always exists for a new project manager, a core team, and management to ask for or add more people or tools. Unfortunately, if the decision to do so is made too early, it could actually aggravate rather than mitigate the project's problems. This decision should be made only after careful analysis and deliberation. A premature decision can cause further delays, add complexity, and impact team performance.

2.6 *Develop a new or revised project charter or statement of work.* The next activity is to develop a new or revised project charter and statement of work, or both. It has to be determined whether the existing vision is feasible under the current circumstances, perhaps with revisions, or whether a new vision should be developed to recover and deliver results efficiently and effectively. The new or revised charter and statement of work should be realistic to avoid disappointing key stakeholder expectations again. It is also important that key stakeholders participate in developing and supporting the new or revised vision.

3.2 2.1: IDENTIFY STAKEHOLDERS

As mentioned earlier, identifying stakeholders is necessary. But this may not be an easy task, for many reasons. Some stakeholders may be people or organizations that are not obviously stakeholders. Not all stakeholders are equal either; some of them have a greater interest in the outcome than others, and they vary in their power to influence results.

Understanding the needs and expectations of key stakeholders is absolutely essential to achieving project success. Without trying to understand needs and expectations, you can have the best project in the world, but it will be deemed a failure despite having finished on time, within budget, and with the highest workmanship.

There are three steps to managing stakeholders effectively.

One, identify them. A key stakeholder can be a person or organization, such as a department or another company. These stakeholders come from a variety of functional areas. Besides you and your team members, stakeholders can come from organizations such as contracts, procurement, engineering, information technology, quality control, and employee relations. These individuals and organizations may participate in one or more of the following generic roles, each with its unique set of responsibilities: sponsor, senior management, customer, project manager, and project team member.

Two, identify the needs and expectations of each stakeholder regarding the project. Answer questions such as "What are his specific interests?" and "How will the stakeholder be impacted by the success or failure of the project?" You can use a stakeholder register to capture answers.

The third and final step is to determine the degree of interest and influence each stakeholder can bring to bear on a project. You can reflect the degree of interest and influence in a quadrant chart, or matrix. The value of the chart is that it forces you and your core team to recognize the political impact on the project and ensure consideration of the needs and expectations of stakeholders.

Here is a list of categories of the most common stakeholders that may or may not be involved with your project. You can break them down into various categories, for example, internal versus external, influential versus noninfluential, and direct interest versus indirect interest. The topical list of stakeholders may include

- Accounts Payable
- Accounts Receivable
- Education and Training
- Engineering
- Facilities
- Finance

- Human Resources or Personnel
- Industrial Engineering and Methods
- Information Technology
- Legal or Law
- Logistics
- Manufacturing
- Office/Administrative Services
- Purchasing
- Quality Assurance or Quality Control
- Research and Development
- Sales and Marketing

The list of organizations can be innumerable, especially with a large entity such as a major corporation or government.

Within each organization is a leadership team (such as first- and second-level managers, directors, and vice presidents); other overhead staff, such as subject matter experts in a specialty discipline; and line people, who run operations. Some or all of these people in each organization may be a stakeholder in your project, either directly or indirectly. You need to identify the key ones and get them engaged to the extent needed to turn around your project.

One of the best ways to start identifying those stakeholders is to get together with your core team and create what is known as a stakeholder log. The log captures some of the basic information about each stakeholder, especially important ones. Figure 3.3 is an example of a stakeholder register, or log.

Of course, not all stakeholders are equal; some have a greater interest or influence than others. You will need to capture that information, too. One of the most convenient ways to do that is to create a four square chart that shows the relationship between two variables, such as interest and power, and plot their respective degrees of importance in that cell. This chart will enable you to determine to what extent a stakeholder gets engaged and in what events or activities.

Figure 3.4 shows an example of a stakeholder four square chart.

The relationship between variables can take many different permutations: power and influence, power and interest, money and interest, etc. You and your core team need to determine what variables are important and then plot them. You can then add this information to the stakeholder log.

Stakeholder Name	Overall Reason for Interest	Specific Interests in Project	When Involved in Project Life Cycle	Ways to Engage

FIGURE 3.3
Stakeholder register.

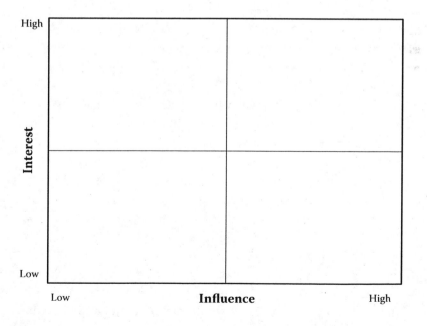

FIGURE 3.4
Stakeholder matrix.

Identifying stakeholders is not always easy, especially the key ones. There may be several reasons for this. One, the scope of the project may be so nebulous that just about any person or organization fits under the title of stakeholder. Two, the visibility of the project could be so high that, even though it is in trouble, people want to be associated with it. Three, some stakeholders, while genuinely having an interest, lack a high profile and, therefore, are not obvious to the team. Finally, some stakeholders, though they are key, do not reveal themselves as stakeholders without seeing how well the project is progressing; naturally, if a project is in trouble, chances are high that they will recede into the background, only to resurface when your project starts turning around.

By sitting with your core team and developing a stakeholder log and a stakeholder matrix, you can start identifying stakeholders and begin developing strategies for dealing with each one during the life cycle of a project.

3.3 2.2: TAKE A SYSTEMS APPROACH

To develop a new or revised vision for the project, you and your core team must understand the existing environment. Taking a systems approach is helpful for understanding the current environment.

A systems approach requires identifying all the external entities (e.g., people and organizations, functions, and business and technical processes) that influence the management and execution of a project. However, it goes one step further; it requires looking at all the relationships between and among the entities and processes.

A systems perspective can take many forms. A data-driven perspective, such as the one used in this book, is one possible perspective. Flow of control is another perspective. Still another perspective is an object-oriented one. Regardless of the perspective, the key is to use it to identify problems and their sources, and determine an effective and efficient way to improve project performance.

This model can take whatever form that you and your core team desire. It can, for example, be a flowchart, a data flow diagram, or an object-oriented model to depict the system. The key is to have one, and it does not have to have great detail; the level of detail is a matter of judgment and comfort.

There are several benefits to taking a systems approach.

First, because a project is a collaborative effort by nature, a systems approach forces you and your core team to look beyond a narrow focus. There is a tendency, especially with technical projects, to look at a project from a specific functional discipline, for example, finance or information technology. This approach precludes making decisions based simply on one perspective. It encourages people to look beyond their comfort zones, thereby lessening the impact of the myopia that is especially present on technical projects. With a systems perspective, people are forced to enlarge their perspectives of their environment.

Second, a systems approach enables people to see the impact of decisions, risks, and issues on all or most processes and stakeholders. Armed with this knowledge, they can act to mitigate their impacts. Additionally, they can also identify instances, decisions, and actions that provide opportunities for improvement. People can then leverage the impact of those opportunities and demonstrate the gains to various stakeholders.

Third, a systems perspective enables you and your core team to determine what is, and what is not, under their circle of control. Most project managers have a narrow circle of control, with decisions and actions constraining freedom. A systems perspective enables them to ascertain the possibility and potential impact of external decisions and actions on their projects. The mere act of looking at potential external decisions and actions allows project managers and their core teams to respond more effectively and efficiently than if they had simply waited for something to happen.

Fourth, and finally, a systemic perspective enables leveraging the opportunities, or positive risks arising from developing a new or revised vision. Too often, the focus on turning around a project becomes identifying the negatives. Yet, a new discovery may be made that a tool or technique that can improve performance was discredited previously. With a systems perspective, you can revisit and implement a new idea or a previously discarded one. A systems perspective, because it looks at components and interactions, can enable you and your core team members to look at opportunities to more objectively ascertain the pros and cons of an idea.

When a system reaches equilibrium, it operates at an optimum level with all processes and elements interacting smoothly. Occasionally, however, a system may start to exhibit problems, when equilibrium degenerates into disequilibrium. The source of this disequilibrium may be internal or external; how a system adapts determines whether the system survives.

By analogy, a project is a system. It consists of processes (for example, building schedules), which require inputs (for example, estimates), which, in turn, create outputs (for example, integrated schedule). Processes involve one or more basic elements. Frequently, these basic elements are people and organizations, data and information, manual and automated systems (acting as a system within a system), and policies, procedures, and techniques.

Ideally, the system performs in a state of equilibrium, operating efficiently and effectively. However, sometimes, due to internal or external complications, a project can move into a state of disequilibrium. If the disequilibrium becomes unmanageable, then the project can deteriorate to the point that it finds itself in trouble.

A systemic perspective requires viewing a project as consisting of several processes. Each process requires one or more inputs to perform a function, which, in turn, produces one or more outputs to another process or entity. The process performs a function, such as transformation or transaction of data.

A project consists of basic elements that contribute to its functioning. These elements, typically rules, methods, tools, techniques, etc., enable processes to perform their function.

All processes interact among each other using these elements. Two key concepts in this regard are interdependence and integration.

The processes and elements of all projects exhibit two characteristics to various degrees. Interdependence means that each process performs autonomously to the degree that it generates output that feeds one or more processes in a system. Integration means that a process has the capability to interact with other processes to achieve the ultimate goal of the system.

The project manager who takes over a project in trouble needs to identify the symptoms of disequilibrium. Some symptoms of disequilibrium on a project include

- Exceeding the budget—the costs exceed what was allocated to the project up to a point in time.
- Inadequate or incomplete data—the measures and the corresponding metrics do not tell the truth about the performance of the project.
- Prevalence of negative conflict—people are not working together.
- Sliding schedule—major milestones are missed.
- Unequal distribution of workload—some resources are doing too much of the work.

3.4 2.3: CONDUCT A GAP ANALYSIS OF WHAT WAS AND WHAT SHOULD HAVE BEEN DONE

One of the most valuable sources of information for making an assessment for this activity and the next one is reviewing the requirements and specifications.

These documents (if they are documented) can provide a wealth of information about what specifically was supposed to have been done. You can use the documents as a baseline to ascertain what has and has not been done and whether what was done has value in moving your project forward to achieving its goals and objectives that, hopefully, was articulated in a charter.

Ideally, the requirements documents should provide specifics on topics such as

- Compliance
- Functionality (specifically clarification of wants versus needs)
- Licensing
- Maintenance
- Pricing
- Quality
- Security
- Support
- Training

Frequently, requirements and specifications are replete with nebulous, ill-defined terminology. These terms may have led to problems of misinterpretation or guesswork that contributed toward getting the project in trouble in the first place. Examples of such terminology include customer satisfaction, fast delivery, ease of use, and many others. This loose use of terminology provides clues to where gaps may exist between expectations and actual delivery to date, leading to frustration and lack of creditability on the part of management and the customer.

When collecting or refining requirements, you will likely face challenges that your predecessor may have also experienced but was unable to overcome. These challenges may include having the customer define what constitutes "value," determining when the capture of requirements is complete and accurate, having the customer speak with one voice, determining priorities among requirements, and validating requirements.

You can deal with these and other challenges effectively by prioritizing requirements, relating requirements to goals and objectives, determining who at the customer end is the authoritative source for requirements, ensuring that baseline requirements have been sufficiently captured; using a modeling technique that people can understand, and avoiding analysis paralysis.

The project expended effort, regardless of effectiveness, to achieve the existing vision. The results obviously were inadequate; otherwise the project would not have got into trouble in the first place, and you would not have been brought on board. Deliverables and other artifacts were likely produced, in part or full, and these constitute evidence that you can use to determine the degree to which the vision was achieved.

This gap analysis is useful for many reasons. First, a gap analysis helps determine the extent to which expectations have fallen short, assuming that they were identified and documented. A review of deliverables and the other artifacts can reveal the number and extent of the gaps. Such an examination will expose specific gaps related to cost, schedule, and quality. You and your core team may discover that they will have to first uncover expectations and then do the necessary gap analysis to perform the examination. This examination should include interviewing key stakeholders and performing a documentation review.

Second, gap analysis encourages communications with key stakeholders. By communicating with these stakeholders who produce deliverables and ones who receive output, you and your core team will discover which expectations fell short and which ones were met. The discussions will illuminate issues, problems, and concerns that were probably never discussed in the first place, and which led to a gap.

Third, conducting a gap analysis will, if the communication is direct and honest, provide ideas for closing the gaps. That's because the likely contributor to the gaps was a failure in communications right from the beginning. You might consider meeting first with individual stakeholders who produced the deliverables and then with the customer, thereby giving you two baselines for comparison.

Fourth, a gap analysis will lead to decisions about trade-offs that might require suboptimization, which is adjusting the expectations surrounding the quality and quantity of deliverables relative to cost and schedule. This scenario is often the case when projects are in recovery mode and the options are limited in terms of flexibility.

Fifth, this step will lay the groundwork for satisfying the needs of the customer. The mere act of performing a gap analysis is an assertion by you and your core team that the customer's needs are important and will be given priority in the recovery plan. Customer satisfaction requires, of course, judgments to be made by both parties regarding what is and what is not important. Turning around a project in trouble will pressure parties to decide on what is now possible and what may possibly be moved to a later delivery, dropped from consideration, or provided in a subsequent release.

Finally, performing the gap analysis will enable the team to make decisions that require focusing on efforts of true value. The analysis will reveal that the gap is the result of people performing activities and building deliverables that failed to contribute directly to goals and objectives. In some cases, it may reveal that gold plating (that is, giving more than what the customer requested) occurred on deliverables.

3.5 2.4: TAKE A SNAPSHOT OF WHAT IS GOING WELL AND NOT SO WELL

This step is closely allied to the preceding step, but with a different focus. The focus here is on the effectiveness of the tasks executed to build the deliverables; in other words, *how*, rather than *what*.

In some cases, the deliverables may have been achieved, but with great effort and rework. The selection of methods, approaches, and techniques may have occurred carelessly, contributing to poor cost and schedule performance. By taking a snapshot that looks at the who, what, when, where, why, and how on a project, your core team may start thinking "outside the box" to contribute new ideas for executing tasks effectively.

Of course, discretion is necessary because it may make little sense to revisit how deliverables were created in the past if rework is unnecessary, similar to accounting for "sunk" costs. A review might, however, might reveal some lessons learned to improve performance.

The level of granularity of a snapshot is a judgment call on the part of you and your core team. Going into great depth might not provide much value, and whereas a more panoramic perspective on tools, techniques, processes, and procedures to avoid slowing the recovery effort might make more sense.

Many benefits attributed to performing a gap analysis apply to taking a snapshot of what is, and what is not, going well. This snapshot may include identifying opportunities for removing non-value-added efforts and improving communications among the key stakeholders.

One benefit worth mentioning is that gap analysis can help identify best practices, which will not only contribute to the rapid turnaround of your project but will also be useful for future projects. Best practices, a much-bandied term, are a set of policies, procedures, tools, and techniques that are adopted to maximize performance consistently and reliably. The ability to identify and apply them enables seizing opportunities to meet the objectives of projects. Many projects adopt best practices because of their major contributions to achieving positive results.

With an understanding of Lean, you may discover some of the general contributors to the problems that have plagued your project in the past. By using the basic principles as a checklist with discussions with stakeholders, you can then start thinking about ways to improve performance. This will prove invaluable when you start generating meaningful options for improving performance in the next action, Explore.

Lean is a manufacturing philosophy consisting of a set of concepts, principles, tools, and practices to improve performance from a supply chain perspective, focusing on the customer by eliminating non-value-added processes, procedures, practices, tasks, etc. The result is a reduction in what the Japanese call *muda*, or waste. You can improve effectiveness and efficiency by applying all or some of the following based on the circumstances of your project.

Are you keeping the customer in the forefront? Under Lean, customer satisfaction is critical to success. Striving to satisfy the customer determines priorities based on goals, objectives, and requirements, which should emanate from the vision. That means constantly asking if the supply chain can be improved from the perspective of the customer. Lean emphasizes the need for "pull" rather than "push," meaning that performance is judged by what product or service the customer wants and when, not the team.

On your project, you might look for opportunities to engage the customer. You can do that by developing an effective communications management plan, establishing measures and metrics that are of value to the customer, and soliciting customer feedback on a regular or ad hoc basis.

Is there a need to reduce cycle time? Cycle time is the time it takes from concept to delivery of a product or service being delivered to the customer. The shorter the cycle time, the better. Coupled with this need to reduce cycle time is the ability to move with velocity, that is, speed and direction, which is achievable by keeping the customer's goals and objectives in the forefront at all times.

Perhaps your project has taken too long to deliver something to the customer, causing significant schedule slides. You can then look for opportunities that could improve cycle time, such as reducing reviews and approvals, adopting more effective testing techniques, or streamlining processes by eliminating redundancy.

Do you need to limit work to capacity? An analogy would be not putting more than five pounds of groceries in a five-pound bag. The cumulative characteristics, that is, knowledge and expertise, of your team will indicate whether it can handle the workload assigned to it. Too frequently, project managers take on a workload that far exceeds their ability or capacity to deliver within a given time frame. This overcapacity may be due to management making unrealistic assignments or the project team being too optimistic or naïve about the work. Whatever the reasons, the workload exceeds the capacity of the team.

As the project manager, you can try and tailor the workload to your team's capacity by using incremental delivery of a product. You can also require an impact analysis whenever the team receives an additional request.

Is there a need to reduce variation? While variation may have its advantages in biological evolution, in the manufacturing sector it can sometimes cause complications. Too much uncontrolled variation can lead to rework, excess inventory, and confusion. To offset the impact of uncontrolled variation, tools such as Six Sigma have been adopted to help reduce dispersion, or variation. On your project, for example, you may be experiencing too much variation. If so, you can offset it by adopting standardized processes, tools, methods, or even methodologies as an effort to reduce variation. The team can then focus on achieving the vision, for example, rather than fighting over which process or tool to use.

Are you maintaining a constant pace? The idea is that rather than have your project moving in fits and starts as on a clogged freeway, it should flow at an even, predictable rate. This rate enables greater certainty about how much will be produced at a specific cost over a specified time period. A project in trouble often limps along in fits and starts, which is reflected in poor planning and rework. To maintain a constant pace on a project, you might consider reducing the size of the deliverables, ensure that everyone follows standardized processes, and have all plans based on the work to be done.

Do you stress the importance of focus? Frequently, in projects in trouble, some people get assigned a set of diversified tasks, while others receive less. The former end up jumping from one different set of tasks to another. This situation causes people to reorient themselves each time they return to an incomplete task, resulting in rework, and more and more incomplete work. The equivalent in Lean is the increasing setup time, when in reality the goal is to reduce its time and frequency. On your project, a likely problem is that some key people are not focusing but spreading themselves too thin. Some ways you might consider dealing with such a problem is to perform resource loading; negotiate with functional managers for more stable team members, for example, those not supporting multiple projects; and encourage greater teaming on tasks, especially when the workload can be shared. Projects on a fast track mode are notorious for spreading people too thin, which, rather than speeding up the project as some people claim it does, can cause a delay.

Are you striving to simplify? Lean stresses the need to reduce complexity. More is not necessarily better, and frequently, at least in manufacturing, it can add to all sorts of waste in terms of cost, time, and other variables.

In Lean the best way to simplify is by removing non-value-added tasks. These tasks are identified through the perspective of the customer. If something does not add value to the customer, then consider the process, tool, procedures, practice, etc. as having little value and, therefore, remove it. For your project, you need to understand the vision and requirements clearly and apply that understanding as a litmus test to ascertain whether some tasks on your project are, in fact, adding value; if not, consider stopping or removing them.

Are you building in quality? For many years, quality was treated as something after the fact. Defects were often detected once they went through the manufacturing process. They were discovered after inspection or when the customer noticed them once the product or service was delivered.

Under Lean, quality is built into the processes of developing a product or service and is not treated as something after the fact. Through reliable measurements and metrics, defects are identified early and resolved. Of course, once in a while defects will get through, but the idea is for you and your core team to find out about them before the customer does.

You and your team might consider adopting some practices from Lean. These may include having team members halt the development of a process after detecting a defect, applying Six Sigma to detect and reduce variation, and continuously seeking involvement and feedback from the customer while developing the product or service.

Do you have balanced teams? In an age of specialization, a tendency exists to create teams of specialists to do work and then hand over their work to another group of specialists to do some more work. This approach causes many problems, such as increasing flow time, causing miscommunication, and adding to overhead. Under Lean, while teams of specialists are used, they are not as isolated; instead, they are assigned to a multifunctional group to produce a subset of the final product or service before being assembled, for example, with the final product. Subteams, or even teams, can be numerous on large projects and programs but are an effective approach to integrating the different disciplines and be responsible in some way for the final product. The "over-the-wall" syndrome begins to fade. These teams are often referred to as integrated product teams, or IPTs.

You may want to establish integrated product teams to improve the interaction and communications on your project. You can do that by creating a work breakdown structure that is reflective of a bill of material (a breakdown of a product in hierarchical form), for example, and assign a multidisciplinary group of team members to the development of a subproduct. You might also consider putting together a comprehensive skills matrix, organization chart, and responsibility assignment matrix (RAM) that reflects an integrated product team arrangement.

Have you instituted measures and metrics? As an old saying goes, that which does not get measured does not get done. Under Lean, measurements and metrics are important to determine any variation from baselines and to ensure adherence to standards. These measurements typically under Lean concentrate around quality and, more specifically, defect rates and cycle time. However, other metrics have significance too, especially when important to the customer, such as those concerning financial management and schedule performance. Measurements and the corresponding metrics also serve as effective ways of obtaining continuous feedback on the fundamental question: how well are we doing?

You will likely need to consider what specific measures and metrics will be of value to you, your team, the customer, and other key stakeholders. These measures and metrics should be collected persistently and consistently in regard to content and timing to ensure their validity and reliability. As the project manager, therefore, you might consider measures and metrics related to earned value and defect rates related to rework as well as output from change boards about changes and burn down of physical counts.

Are you concentrating on the top priorities? Based on the feedback of the customer, Lean emphasizes the need to concentrate on what is important first, and only later, on items of less significance. To treat everything as equal dissipates the team's energies and leads to conflict among stakeholders. As mentioned earlier, focus is critical to Lean.

A project in trouble often lacks focus because the team is constantly reacting rather than pro-acting. Everyone has his head down, and no one is stopping to raise his head and ask: Is what we are doing adding value for the customer? The answer may be *no*, even though there may be considerable activity. If your project suffers from this state of affairs, consider instituting effective change management to preclude gold plating (adding more than what the customer asks for); periodically revisiting the vision, goals, and objectives with the customer; and instituting checkpoint, or gate, reviews after the completion of each phase to verify that what was done satisfies the vision, goals, and objectives of the project.

3.6 2.5: DO NOT ADD MORE RESOURCES—NOT JUST YET

People frequently seem to think that the solution to most projects in trouble is to add more people or increase other resources, for example, money and tools. The problem is that this approach could aggravate the very circumstances that caused the trouble in the first place. More is not necessarily better; sometimes, as the saying goes, the cure can be worse than the disease.

Several reasons exist as to why people want to add more resources at this point in time.

Management, along with the project manager, sees this as an opportunity for empire building. More resources can mean more visibility and greater importance.

Another reason is the implied assumption that the current team members are jaded or incompetent. Better resources will alleviate this problem, goes the prevailing belief. Unfortunately, if the management and processes were more effective and efficient in the first place, the likelihood of the project being in trouble due to resources would be low. A strong tendency exists to blame the existing team when the responsibility for troubles may lie elsewhere.

The best approach is to hold off from adding resources. Allow inquiries and fact finding to work themselves out first to define the exact problems, and then develop one or more solutions to address them. Too often, the tendency is to jump to a solution before defining a problem, thereby forcing the latter onto the former. A mismatch can occur, introducing problems far more serious than the original one. The result is a new round of finger pointing, lack of cooperation (exemplified through resistance), and fear. The key is to think before taking a knee-jerk approach. Adding resources at this point in time is an example of a knee-jerk approach that may worsen the problems.

Adding more resources may, in fact, increase communications problems and make the learning curve steeper. Current team members may find they have to temporarily halt their work to train new team members. Adding new capabilities such as tools and techniques will require additional time to learn and increase setup times. Adding more resources can disrupt the norms of the existing team, which, if not handled correctly, may be counterproductive.

To see the impact of adding more people, consider this formula: $[N(N-1)]/2$, where N is the number of people on a project. Using the formula, you can determine the number of communication channels. For example, you have 12 people. You therefore have 66 channels of communications: $[12(12-1)]/2$.

If you decide to add 10 more people right away, you now have 231 channels, almost quadrupling the number of communications channels.

The consequences are clear. If you add more "heads" too quickly, by not preparing them for their involvement in advance, you can cause further delays, confusion, and conflict. The conclusion is that more is not necessarily better; it can—without much forethought and preparation—create even more trouble for your project.

It is clear, therefore, that there are benefits to avoiding adding more people or capabilities. It keeps the team small, especially the core team. Smaller teams tend to work together better than large ones. As a team becomes larger, coordination and communications channels multiply, resulting in a higher level of complexity. The threshold for reaching a higher level of complexity depends on many factors, for example, technology, skill levels, and schedule. Generally, more people and more capabilities cause greater complexity. Contrary to contemporary thinking, complexity is not equivalent to thorough, clear thinking; it often reflects the opposite.

By avoiding adding more people or capabilities, a project can also avoid "collapsing under its own weight." Adding more resources may cause a project to implode, resulting in further degradation in cost, quality, and schedule performance. It's equivalent to putting one hundred pounds of groceries in a five pound bag; sooner or later the capacity of the bag will reach its threshold and burst. To repeat: avoid adding more resources, especially people, until the project manager and the core team determine the necessary requirements for recovery.

3.7 2.6: DEVELOP A NEW OR REVISED PROJECT CHARTER

Many people on projects have no idea what the goals and objectives are for their project. Instead, they perform Kentucky windage: Take general aim and fire, and hopefully they will hit something when firing in the approximate direction of the target. This scenario is all too common. The consequences play a large role in causing a project to quickly fall into trouble.

Because projects are people intensive, the danger increases dramatically that individuals can resemble different-colored marbles that spill to the floor and scatter in multiple directions. This results in rework, waste, and nonproductive behavior.

A vision, new or revised, helps to offset this tendency to scatter. People understand what they are supposed to achieve as they collaborate with each other.

The mere act of discussing the vision can pay considerable dividends for the project. It opens opportunities for stakeholders to communicate among each other about their project-related issues. It encourages underlying problems and fears to emerge sooner rather than later, allowing an early opportunity to address them. Waiting too late in the life cycle to discuss issues can jeopardize achieving results.

There are two additional, perhaps more important, benefits of building a new or revised charter. It builds bridges rather than walls among stakeholders. As just mentioned, it provides an opportunity for stakeholders to start a dialogue that apparently was missing earlier. Of course, this requires considerable effort from you because the hard feelings generated earlier may resurface. If that does happen, good. Allowing feelings to resurface releases pent-up resentment that is smoldering and, if left unattended, could erupt at an inopportune time.

It also provides the basis for generating a new set of plans. A new or revised vision lays the groundwork for building a reliable, solid recovery plan. The contents of the vision will enable the team to focus on what is important from the perspective of the stakeholder. It also draws the parameters or boundaries of what the team can or should not consider when building plans, for example, work breakdown structure (WBS) and schedule.

The charter is a document that helps to define, both in business and technical terms, what the project is to achieve. Although a high-level document, it provides a guide that all subsequent plans and actions are predicated upon. The high-level technical descriptions are often contained in a separate or appended statement of work (SOW).

Whether you are developing a new or revised charter for your project, you can expect some challenges.

The first challenge is likely to be the one that got the project in trouble initially—caving in to unrealistic requests by senior management or the customer. These unrealistic requests may require a schedule that had no bearing on the work to be done, understating financial needs to satisfy immediate budget requirements, agreeing to quality standards that are impractical under the current circumstances, or taking on a larger-than-practical scope simply to get permission to proceed.

The second challenge is the danger of incorporating unclear, ambiguous phrases into the narrative of the charter. Words such as customer satisfaction or delivering a turnkey system appear nice and hard to argue with, but in reality they are meaningless, unless, of course, the terms are well defined and have concrete success criteria supporting them. Failure to define such terminology only tends to raise expectations, perhaps unrealistically, leading to misunderstandings and disappointment.

The third challenge is obtaining information that can help you develop a charter. The likelihood is strong that you will have either too much or too little data, but that is only part of the problem. The other part is converting that data into something meaningful, that is, information. Assuming you will be the one drafting the charter and not the project sponsor, you will need to pull information from different sources, memoranda, studies, business cases, and portfolios to extract what you need to complete the charter. However, that is not enough. You will also have to get the input and feedback from key stakeholders to ensure buy-in for the charter once it has been drafted, approved, and released.

Finally, you will need to identify all risks and constraints, which is a task that is easier said than done. Some constraints and risks will be obvious, such as ones related to cost, schedule, and quality. However, the more subtle ones, such as political support, are less tangible but just as important to identify and should be reflected in the charter. The only problem is that it is hard to articulate them, and they are sometimes too sensitive to identify in the charter.

The best way to overcome these challenges is for you to avoid developing the charter unilaterally. It is fine to put a straw horse together but ultimately the key stakeholders need to be the real authors of the document. Without their input and buy-in, you could find yourself facing considerable resistance the minute you start managing and leading your team.

There are many reasons why a charter has shortcomings. The key stakeholders may be procrastinators, indecisive, or unengaged. Or, the data and information to construct the charter is incomplete, inaccurate, or unavailable.

You must act as soon as possible to develop or revise a charter. Some quick approaches are for you to produce a straw horse and solicit feedback from key stakeholders, document concerns about the shortcomings and record them as risks, or assemble stakeholders at a common venue to draft or revise a charter.

The charter should pay particular attention to scope definition. This requires defining the "boundaries" of your project. An excellent approach to defining the scope is to identify what is not included, thereby helping to more clearly articulate what is in the scope. An appended statement of work or draft of a scope document can clarify shortcomings on what is and what is not in scope.

It should identify how the project ties in with the strategic direction of the parent organization. Specifically, it should describe how the project aligns with the missions, goals, objectives, and operational plans.

Another key topic to address is the goals and objectives of the project. Not only will this help determine alignment with the parent organization, but it will also let key stakeholders know what specifically to accomplish. Goals are statements of intent, such as "build a state-of-the-art inventory system." They tend to be general in nature, but are not sufficiently articulated enough to indicate when that goal has been reached. That's where objectives become necessary.

Objectives are measurable criteria that, having been attained, tell the project manager and other key stakeholders that the goal has been attained. The building of a state-of-the-art inventory system, for example, should be supported with tangible objectives such as "The system will support 30 workstations," "The system will have less than 35,000 lines of code," or "The system will have a response time of less than 2 seconds."

Goals can have one or more objectives; one objective can support more than one goal. To be meaningful to key stakeholders, an objective should satisfy the famous SMART acronym: *S*pecific, *M*easurable, *A*chievable, *R*ealistic, and *T*ime-bound.

Here are some additional topics to address in the new or revised charter:

- Assumptions: Suppositions or perceptions assumed to be facts until proved otherwise
- Budget: The overall costs of supporting the project
- Constraints: Conditions that restrict the options of the team, such as cost or schedule constraints
- Deliverables: The interim and final items produced as a result of the efforts of the project team
- Responsibilities: Who performs what high-level tasks
- Risk: Future scenarios or events that, should they occur, could alter the course or progress of the project
- Schedule: Significant milestones or red-letter dates to meet
- Signatures: The signatures of optional key stakeholders indicate their commitment to stand by the charter

One of the best sources of information for determining the expectations and perhaps the original vision for your project is the business case that was developed to determine whether to proceed with the project. That is, of course, if a business case was done. Assuming it was, you can use the content in your conversations with stakeholders. Here are some topics to look for in the business case and the reasons why they are important.

Tangible and nontangible justifications. All benefits to be realized should have been articulated clearly in the business case. Some benefits are tangible, that is, quantifiable; for example, a positive return on investment (ROI). Other benefits may be nonquantifiable, for example, improving customer satisfaction. Identifying these benefits can help you sit with your customer and other key stakeholders to determine whether they are still relevant or need revision; you can also use them to develop a new or revised charter.

Assumptions. All business cases, if done correctly, are based on assumptions. These assumptions are assumed to be true until evidence to the contrary turns up. Circumstances may have negated some assumptions and reinforced others. You need to determine which assumptions fall under which circumstance. The reason is that assumptions have a substantial influence on the scope and choice of options in your recovery plans.

Calculations. Review the calculations for the business case. Determine what values and assumptions were used to perform calculations. Were the data used for variables accurate? Were the assumptions relevant and valid? For example, when the ROI was calculated, was it based on net present value (NPV)? Were the assumptions used in both ROI and NPV calculations realistic at the time and, perhaps more so, useful now? Can the same be said of the payback period and cost-benefit ratio calculations, too? This information is useful when discussing with stakeholders about expectations and making recovery plans to match those expectations or making revisions to the latter accordingly.

Sources of information. Look at the business case to determine the sources of information needed to conduct it. Were the sources credible? Was "politics" an overriding influence on the outcome of the business case? Knowing the sources of information will help you determine just how credible the information and the results of the business case really are. You can then use that information to position the recovery plan for acceptance by key stakeholders. You may even have to suggest that a new business case be done.

Criteria for evaluation. If the business case is considered at different options, look at each criterion used in the decision making. Were the criteria complete? Were the criteria relevant? You may find that the option chosen was based on faulty assumptions and data. You may find that the criteria were applied inconsistently. You may find terminology used that was not clearly defined, requiring the use of too many assumptions rather than facts and data.

Selling of your project. Call it politics or whatever you like, but a project could have been oversold to key stakeholders. Your project may have come into being because of the influence of a senior executive or to placate a government authority. Whatever the reason, the rationale for the project may not be based on rationality at all, that is, based on facts, data, and logic. The business case is often done to justify a project, and you need to uncover whether the justification is sound. This information will enable you to leverage the politics to gain new support for your recovery plan.

As with a business case, one of the best sources of information about the rationale for your project is content, or your organization's project portfolio—assuming, of course, that one exists.

Strategic alignment. A good portfolio will indicate how well your project aligns with the strategic direction of your organization. For example, it should tell you what corporate and departmental goals and strategies it supports. If your project does not support one or more of the higher-level goals and objectives, that could explain why the project is in trouble in the first place and will indicate just how important your project is to the organization.

Priority relative to other projects. After reviewing the portfolio, you should be able to determine the ranking of importance of your project relative to other projects. A number of factors should have gone into this determination, such as net present value, return on investment, strategic fit, payback period, etc. By knowing how your project ranks relative to other projects, you will have an idea of what stakeholders feel about your project. This information will be important when you start to negotiate for additional resources.

Criteria for ranking. The outcome of the ranking will largely be determined by the criteria used and the weighting of each criterion. By knowing the criteria and the weighting, you can then attempt to reposition your project in trouble in such a way that it will fare better if the ranking is redetermined. This information will enable you to start repositioning your project so that you can obtain additional support from key stakeholders, who will begin to see the project in a different light.

Participation in portfolio. As with many other aspects, politics can influence how a portfolio is viewed. It may be that powerful executives had a significant influence on the outcome of the portfolio and that your project was important but did not have a strong enough sponsor. You need to know this, so that whenever you need to recover your project in trouble, you can seek a more important ally or sponsor.

Otherwise, without an ally, you can find your project once again in trouble regardless of how well planned your recovery plans are.

You may find that whether developing a new or revised charter, you will face challenges, which you should be aware of to preclude problems later in the life cycle of your project. These challenges include acquiescing to unrealistic requests and unclear phrases and terminology; lack of information; no, or minimal, participation; and lack of commitment by certain key stakeholders.

To address these challenges, you can take action that will help eliminate or alleviate the impact of these challenges: set up group sessions, solicit input to drafts of the charter, give visibility to progress, and bring to the forefront potential shortcomings in the content of the charter.

3.8 CONCLUSION

The essence of Envision is to get the right stakeholders together to determine whether the existing vision is sufficient or whether it needs revision or replacement. The basis for that decision is to look at previous work, both from a qualitative and perhaps quantitative perspective, and then identify the gap between expectations and reality. The magnitude of the gap will determine the extent of the change required in the vision. This approach precludes the common tendency to react by adding resources. Instead, the focus shifts to the vision first, which lays the groundwork for all recovery actions, including the adding of more resources to the project as demonstrated in the other actions discussed in this book.

Case Study (*Continued*)

Envision. Although Deborah had a good idea who the key stakeholders were, she needed to conduct a further review, especially for attendance at the three-day off-site meeting. The key questions were: Who should be invited, why should they be invited, and what were their interests in the project? Working with her core team, she developed a stakeholder register that captured the necessary information.

Prior to the meeting, she prepared the ground for a successful outcome. She met with some members of the core team and management to determine the agenda, assigned someone to be the scribe, and decided to facilitate the session herself. The agenda was sent out ahead of time for people to prepare for the meeting; she also verified with management and the representatives from the internal customer if the right stakeholders had been invited.

To get a better understanding of the application to be built, Deborah decided that she needed to map out the original vision of the product to be built on the first day. It had become apparent in her one-on-one sessions that no one really had an understanding of the big picture of what the final product should do or look like. After reviewing the original charter and smattering of documents that could be construed as a statement of work, she had the team put up on the walls in a large room a roll of butcher paper. With a pen in hand, she asked the core team to help her draw a diagram explaining the capabilities, functions, data requirements, and their relationship to one another. Immediately, team members experienced what can only be described as an epiphany. For the first time, they had a truly holistic understanding of what would constitute a large part of the vision for the project.

With everyone on the team focused on the chart, Deborah was able to take a systemic view of the application. With this knowledge, she and the team then proceeded to determine what was done to date and what should have been done to date, as well what had been going well and not so well. Although some of the people said they needed more developers, she was able to ask them to hold off until the session moved into the planning stage; eventually, as a side note, it was determined that they could actually achieve the vision with two fewer developers.

Once everyone had gained an understanding of the product to be built, she asked the team to help her review the charter as they understood it. After some in-depth discussions, she captured revisions based on the core team's feedback as well as a number of suggestions for improving work processes and improving product capabilities. The representatives from the internal customer agreed with many of the suggestions, as well as with the charter. Deborah emphasized that the steering team would have to approve the revisions and that she would communicate those revisions to it.

3.9 GETTING-STARTED CHECKLIST

Question	Yes	No
1. Will you identify stakeholders?	___	___
If so, will you		
Distinguish between direct and indirect stakeholders?	___	___
Distinguish between internal versus external stakeholders?	___	___
Distinguish between influential versus noninfluential stakeholders?	___	___
Understand their needs and expectations?	___	___
Determine their degree of interest and influence?	___	___
2. Are any of your stakeholders from the following areas:		
Accounts Payable?	___	___
Accounts Receivable?	___	___
Education and Training?	___	___
Engineering?	___	___
Facilities?	___	___
Finance?	___	___
Human Resources and Personnel?	___	___
Industrial Engineering or Methods?	___	___
Information Technology?	___	___
Legal or Law?	___	___
Logistics?	___	___
Manufacturing?	___	___
Office/Administrative Services?	___	___
Purchasing?	___	___
Quality Assurance or Quality Control?	___	___
Research and Development?	___	___
Sales and Marketing?	___	___
3. Will you create a stakeholder log?	___	___
4. Will you develop a stakeholder four square chart?	___	___
5. Will you take a systems approach?	___	___
If so, did you identify		
Entities, for example, people, organizations?	___	___
Processes, for example, building a schedule?	___	___
Relationships, for example, among stakeholders?	___	___
Data, for example, earned value metrics?	___	___
6. Is there a danger that any of the following potential causes of idea squashing exist:		
Groupthink?	___	___
Ostracism?	___	___
Mind guards?	___	___

Question	Yes	No
Organizational culture?	____	____
Economic conditions?	____	____
Mental filtering?	____	____
Not listening?	____	____
Positive incentives?	____	____
Negative incentives?	____	____
Apathy?	____	____
Your behavior?	____	____
Ego?	____	____
Tendency toward action?	____	____
7. When generating ideas, do you use de Bono's Hat Thinking?	____	____
Brainstorming?	____	____
Mind mapping?	____	____
Critical thinking?	____	____
Minimize emotion?	____	____
8. Will you conduct a gap analysis of what was and what should have been done?	____	____
9. Does the requirements document address topics like		
Security?	____	____
Functionality?	____	____
Training?	____	____
Support?	____	____
Maintenance?	____	____
Compliance?	____	____
Quality?	____	____
Pricing?	____	____
Licensing?	____	____
10. Will you take a snapshot of what is going well and not so well?	____	____
11. Have you considered the following Lean concepts, principles, tasks, and practices?		
Keep the customer in the forefront	____	____
Reduce cycle time	____	____
Limit work to capacity	____	____
Reduce variation	____	____
Maintain a constant pace	____	____
Stress the importance of forms	____	____
Strive to simplify	____	____
Build in quality	____	____
Establish balanced teams	____	____

Question	Yes	No
Institute measures and metrics	____	____
12. Will you avoid the tendency to add more resources immediately?	____	____
Will you develop a new or revised statement of understanding or charter?	____	____
13. Are you aware of the following challenges on your project when developing a new or revised charter?		
Caving in to unrealistic requests	____	____
Incorporating unclear, unambiguous phrases	____	____
Obtaining information that can help you develop a charter	____	____
Identifying all risks and constraints	____	____
14. Does the new or revised charter		
Pay particular attention to scope definition?	____	____
Identify how the project ties in with the strategic direction of the parent organization?	____	____
Address the goals and objectives of the project?	____	____
Provide measurable completion criteria?	____	____
List assumptions?	____	____
Identify responsibilities?	____	____
List deliverables?	____	____
Identify constraints?	____	____
Indicate budget?	____	____
Provide significant milestones?	____	____
Identify high-level risks?	____	____
Provide space for signatures of key stakeholders?	____	____
15. When referring to the business case, do you review the		
Tangible and nontangible justifications?	____	____
Assumptions?	____	____
Calculations?	____	____
Sources of information?	____	____
Criteria for evaluation?	____	____
Selling of the project?	____	____

4

Explore

4.1 AN OVERVIEW

With the vision in place, whether accepted as is or revised, you are now ready to turn ideas into reality by taking the next action, Explore, shown in Figure 4.1. However, you cannot do this alone. Input is required from stakeholders, especially team members. This entire action is focused on obtaining their ideas, input, and feedback.

The basic premise is that the people who do the work know the best way to achieve the vision. At this point, you can start engaging with the rest of the team, not just the core team members. The vision is now in place from which subsequent actions and activities emanate. You have to have a basis for communicating with all team members about meaningful change.

Many benefits are attributed to this viewpoint. One, it builds commitment. Individuals with responsibilities for executing part of a vision will likely have more emotional ownership than someone who merely takes orders and follows directions. It becomes their responsibility, not that of the project manager pontificating from a distance.

Two, as mentioned earlier, the people who do the work often know best how to make a success of it. A team member can use his or her knowledge, expertise, and insights to determine the best approach or way to achieve the vision, goals, and objectives.

Three, it relies on knowledge about the mistakes, errors, and successes of the past. The individuals who did the actual work, even if they got the project in trouble in the first place, have valuable experience that can provide great insights into improvement opportunities and background information. A wise project manager will tap that resource. One tool is lessons learned that leverage past experience to improve future performance.

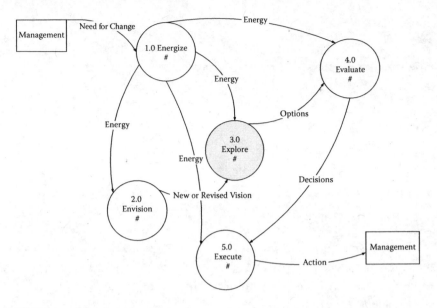

FIGURE 4.1
Level One Overview: Explore.

Explore is looking at all the available options to turn a troubled project into a successful endeavor by leveraging experiences and knowledge of the team and other key stakeholders.

There are five key activities for executing this action (shown in Figure 4.2):

3.1 Get people to share feelings and information.
3.2 Recognize that everyone's interests are important.
3.3 Get people to think about the project's state and suggest improvements.
3.4 Remove non-value-added work.
3.5 Identify options.

Although the activities do not necessarily occur sequentially, they are presented as such for simplicity. In reality, the first three steps are often addressed at the same time, either in one-on-one sessions or at a group meeting or both.

3.1 *Get people to share feelings and information.* The first activity is to get people to share their emotions, insights, and information about the

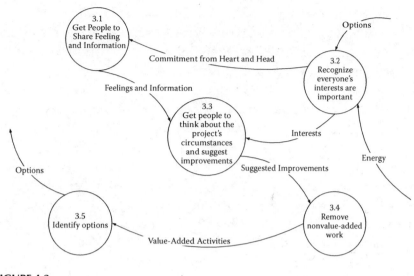

FIGURE 4.2
Level Two: Explore.

project based on their past experience and their perceptions about the future. A major goal is for you to start bonding with team members to build confidence and trust throughout the project. During both individual and group sessions, you should strive to understand their general attitude to the current situation and compile previously acquired information from the previous Envision action.

3.2 *Recognize that everyone's interests are important.* The key goal here is to recognize that people participate in projects for many reasons and not necessarily for the vision. You should achieve a win-win relationship between the needs of team members and those of the project. By building a symbiotic relationship, you and your team members can increase the likelihood of greater productivity and performance. Essentially, you are creating a "marriage" between the head and the heart of the individuals in the pursuit of a project's goals and objectives.

3.3 *Get people to think about the project's circumstances and suggest improvements.* After building effective communications and getting team members to see that their own success is tied with the project's, you can start soliciting suggestions to overcome past problems and identify ways to achieve the vision. Rapport, either on an individual or team basis, is very important to generate meaningful ideas. Again, the philosophy here is that people who do the work can best provide insights on improvements and how to implement them. You should work on building relationships and creating the circumstances to facilitate their participation.

3.4 *Remove non-value-added work.* This activity is deeper than the previous one. This time you use the information obtained from the team and put a stop to tasks not contributing to the vision. This activity should occur daily and require follow-up by team members.

3.5 *Identify options.* This activity consists of compiling information obtained from key stakeholders, including team members, and identifying options to realize the new vision. These options may vary in number and category. The options provide the basis to perform the next action, Evaluate.

4.2 3.1: GET PEOPLE TO SHARE FEELINGS AND INFORMATION

Problems can span many issues, from cost, schedule, quality, and scope to technical and human performance. They can happen at any time and in any situation. A troubled project is replete with problems.

There are two good reasons, therefore, to identify and address problems up front.

A problem left unattended now will likely become bigger later in the project life cycle and especially at a time when you least need it. Denying that a problem exists or feigning ignorance of it will only make matters worse. Chances are good that a problem will resurface with a vengeance at the wrong time, such as just before the delivery of a product or service, causing a slide in a major milestone.

The other reason is cost. Denying or ignoring a problem will make it more costly to address later; this is especially true of technical problems. As a problem becomes more acute, perhaps even "under the radar," it can transform from a minor nuisance to a showstopper. Extensive overtime and the purchase of expensive consultants are two examples that can drive costs up to unexpected levels.

Addressing problems requires good interpersonal skills, and when recovering a project, you have to be at your best. People need to feel comfortable enough with you to start a dialogue, which is not as easy as it may seem, for several reasons.

One, people on a team may regard you as an intruder. Although management and the customer may have felt uncomfortable about the project, the team members may have been loyal to the previous project manager. This situation, therefore, must be dealt with in such a way that dialogue can start and, just as importantly, continue through the life of a project.

Two, people may have been used to working independently and may find the new disciplined approach difficult to tolerate. They may agree in principle with the new approach to the project, but when it is applied directly to them, they feel differently. Good, ongoing dialogue is important to deal with issues confronting a project.

Three, people may be reluctant to express negative feelings. Some individuals prefer to avoid unpleasant topics, though a project manager is expected to raise them early and quickly. Failure to do so can lead to negative feelings surfacing dramatically at an awkward point in the project life cycle. Once again, you should strive to build a dialogue no matter how difficult the experience.

Good dialogue gives stakeholders an opportunity to share feelings and information, which in turn offers several benefits.

One, it causes issues to arise early on, especially emotional ones. People have an opportunity to express themselves, giving you a data point to determine the expected degree of cooperation from other stakeholders.

Two, if the interaction goes well, you can start to build trust and credibility with team members. This trust and credibility will, in turn, ease the sharing of feelings and information. Of course, the feelings and information shared with you should be kept confidential unless otherwise noted. Failure to do so will stop dialogue as the trust and credibility will likely dissolve immediately and cause substantial interaction problems among stakeholders.

Three, the sharing of feelings and information will give you a sense of the magnitude of challenges facing you and the support you will get when implementing changes. You can then proactively cause change by using it as a data point to develop ways of overcoming resistance that you will likely face.

You can take one of three approaches to sharing feelings and information. One-on-one sessions with individual team members work best. Much depends on the size and geographical spread of the team, of course, but one-on-one sessions allow an intimacy that permit people to open up in a way that would otherwise be impossible within a group.

It is best to hold one-on-one sessions in a quiet, private location. These sessions should occur in a relaxed, nonintrusive manner, away from noise and interruptions. The focus should be on interaction and purpose. Above all, the content of these sessions should be kept confidential. If you plan to compile this information, you should let the person know and assure him or her of confidentiality.

Group sessions are another approach. The advantages are that they can save time, money, and effort, at least in the immediate future. The downsides are that a group session can inhibit free flow of emotions and information, due largely to peer pressure. It can also deteriorate into fierce disagreements, resulting in recriminations and verbal hostility.

A combination of one-on-one and group sessions seems to work best. The former allows for privacy to share feelings and information, while the latter offers a way to share that information in a compiled form. It is during the group session that the pros and cons of alternative courses of action can be further discussed, and what the project manager learned can be verified. Again, it is important to maintain the confidentiality of all one-on-one sessions.

To effectively Execute, you need to stress the importance of having open communication, both vertically and laterally, with all stakeholders. Vertical communication is up and down the chain of command; horizontal communication is peer to peer.

In the movie *Cool Hand Luke*, there is famous line by one of the characters that sums up what often occurs on projects that are headed for trouble: "What we have here is a failure to communicate." Many projects have more than their fair share of this type of failure, leading to the question, why is failure to communicate so common?

One reason is that the leadership of the team, often the project sponsor and the project manager, wants to minimize communications from team members. It already has made up its mind, and any communication is either greeted with a "Thank you very much, now get back to work" or "We'll ask for your opinion when we want it" attitude. It simply wants team members to follow orders, and nothing more.

Another reason is fear: fear of being retaliated against, fear of being humiliated, fear of being wrong, or fear of being a scapegoat if something goes wrong. This fear can be realized in both overt and subtle ways. For example, an overt form of retaliation is being fired from the project; a subtle one is not being invited to key meetings or being excluded from key correspondence.

You need to establish and maintain good communication, starting the minute you arrive. A key tool to promote good communications is applying active listening.

Ironically, active listening is the best communication tool you can employ, in which the other person does most of the talking. As an active listener, you get together with key stakeholders and learn as much about the project as possible by following listening principles, such as

- Concentrate: for example, do not look out the window while the other person is talking.
- Empathizing, not sympathizing: for example, trying to see the situation from the speaker's perspective.
- Focusing on the message: for example, asking for clarifications to improve understanding.
- Maintaining eye contact: for example, showing you are paying attention by looking at the person as he or she speaks.
- Not interrupting except to clarify a point: for example, let the person have his or her say before you speak.
- Staying on topic: for example, not changing the subject.
- Watching body language: for example, looking for potential signs of defensiveness.

A good understanding of the communication process helps, too. For communication to happen, a sender and receiver must be involved. The sender creates the message and transmits it over a medium; the receiver decodes and interprets it. The sender then codes the message and sends it back as feedback to the receiver. Ideally, the transaction goes smoothly. In reality, however, noise, or interference, gets in the way, leading to misinterpretation and hostility. This noise can be due to technological factors, but more often than not, to human factors; here, noise consists of emotions, beliefs, values, mores, paradigms, etc. These human factors can result in miscoding and mis-decoding of messages, resulting in a partial or biased interpretation of the message, on either the sender's or receiver's part.

When trying to determine the cause of a problem, you may find that communication with key stakeholders can become quite difficult because of all the noise generated in the past and currently being generated. Here are some actions that you can take to help circumvent the noise that hampers effective communication on your project:

- Ask questions to uncover the cause of a problem, not just the symptoms; look for the whys and not just the hows.
- Consider alternative points of view; remember that diversity of thought is just as important as diversity of race, religion, etc.
- Recognize that noise exists, and account for it when listening to the stakeholder; consider the contexts of the project's past and present situation.
- Seek positive disagreement, not negative conflict, to bring out useful insights and information; differences are fine as long as they don't get personal.
- Segregate facts and data from assumptions and opinions; separate fact from fiction based on objective analysis.

4.3 3.2: RECOGNIZE EVERYONE'S INTERESTS ARE IMPORTANT

Everyone joins a project team for a reason. Some are motivated by money, others by a challenge, and still others want to broaden their experience. More often than not, you have to take the initiative to find out why people are on your project.

This information is critical to help you motivate and retain people who can help you recover the project. The idea is that if you can satisfy their need, they will contribute more. Here are some reasons why people join a project.

Some people may join for psychological satisfaction. They may find that a difficult project challenges them. They may see it as an opportunity to self-actualize or perhaps gain sociological satisfaction.

Other people may join because they see a project as an opportunity to enhance their career. A high-visibility project, even if it is in trouble, gives them access to people and career ladders that can help propel them forward, either inside or outside the organization.

Still other people may join a project to increase their knowledge and expertise. Any project, whether or not it is in trouble, can offer opportunities to learn new tools and techniques or acquire experience that individuals can leverage elsewhere.

Finally, people may join a project to increase their income. Frequently, a project in recovery mode is an opportunity to make more money. They may be hired on the project at a higher pay due to their expertise, or they can work overtime.

Knowing why people join a project is critical because there is an issue of expectations and synchronicity. Under expectations theory, people expect certain needs to be fulfilled, and failure to satisfy them may lead to their departure or declining productivity. Under the principle of synchronicity, if you can match the work assigned with the needs of the individual, hopefully the result will be a happier team member. By satisfying both expectations and synchronicity, it is more likely that people will become committed because you have addressed the timeless acronym: WIIFM (What's In It For Me).

Knowing the reasons will enable you to develop a win-win relationship with team members. You can, for instance, have a person work on a task that helps satisfies his or her psychological need. When that need is satisfied, the team member becomes more productive and works better with other team members to generate synergy.

Another benefit is that a more satisfied team member will likely increase morale and esprit de corps of the team. Satisfied team members tend to interact and integrate with colleagues more positively.

The final benefit is that people will view their interests as being in line with the project's and, consequently, be inclined to share ideas on improving project performance. Hence, if the project succeeds, you will too.

The key is to build positive relationships among team members, thereby allowing you to focus on implementing the vision of the project.

4.4 3.3: GET PEOPLE TO THINK ABOUT THE PROJECT'S CIRCUMSTANCES AND SUGGEST IMPROVEMENTS

Creativity, described here as acting to change or improve the way of doing business to achieve a vision, is critical for successfully turning around a project in trouble.

Yet, nothing is more difficult to do on a project in trouble than encouraging creative thinking. Key stakeholders, especially team members, are likely to have suffered negative experiences. Not surprisingly, fear—over rejection, failure, being targeted, ostracized, or fired—can kill the creative spirit both on an individual and team basis.

Often, a team member proposes a new idea for improving the performance of a project and it gets squashed as quickly as it arises, only for it to emerge later that the idea was the right one in the first place. "Idea squashing" is common on a project in trouble because the atmosphere is so toxic and the hopelessness so dire that team members keep their ideas to themselves. Here are some common causes and ways ideas get squashed on a project:

Groupthink. The peer pressure gets so immense that not only do the team members collude to maintain an illusion of reality, but they feel compelled to keep ideas to themselves.

Ostracism. This effect is aligned closely to groupthink; team members expressing an unpopular or different idea are banished from the group either permanently or through subtle ways like omitting them from key meetings or dropping them from important messages, for example, significant e-mails.

Mind guards. These individuals, often self-appointed, are the guardians of determining what is or is not the right way of thinking or behaving. They assume the responsibility of being the policeman for dismissing thoughts contrary to the status quo. Their power is based either on appearance, knowledge, expertise, personality, or some other factor.

Organizational culture. The overall culture of the organization can inhibit ideas. People will be reluctant to express an idea that some powerful people would not likely embrace or that violates the tone at the top.

Economic conditions. When a downturn in the economy occurs, the time for generating new ideas is never more critical. Yet, the pressure to inhibit ideas is never stronger. People are reluctant to come up with a new idea that may seem controversial for fear of becoming targeted for dismissal or some other retribution. Perhaps worse, the project adopts the idea, and still the individual finds himself targeted.

Mental filtering. This can occur either on an individual or group level. The mental paradigm that dominates provides an orderly way of thinking, but it can also prove dangerous to new ideas. It can filter out information and ideas that do not align with its fundamental beliefs, norms, values, etc. Anything inconsistent with the paradigm is discarded.

Not listening. Some teams are so set in their ways and thoughts that any ideas, however valuable, are ignored. Not listening is often the result of challenges currently discussed in this section. Ironically, applying effective and active listening skills is an excellent way to counteract the effects of groupthink, mental filtering, mind guards, and others.

Positive incentives. Even a positive atmosphere can inhibit the generation of new ideas. A good idea may end up upsetting the status quo, especially for those individuals who have the most to lose because of it. It's hard to understand that a project can get into trouble because people are fearful of jeopardizing a good situation. The result is that any idea that even has the appearance of upsetting the status quo becomes suspect. Too much of a "good thing" can lead to schedule slides, cost overruns, and poor output.

Negative incentives. This one, of course, is the opposite of positive incentives. Negative incentives, such as lost pay and the threat of formal removal from the team, inhibit people from offering good ideas. The pain exceeds the benefits from the new ideas.

Apathy. No one cares about the project. People on the team might be on it just because they were told to participate and had no other option but to accept. Others may be on the project because it is a stepping stone to something more in line with their interests. Whatever the reason, someone who provides an idea simply gets ignored and withers away because he or she is the only one who cares.

Your behavior. As a project manager, you too can inhibit idea generation. Psychologically, physically, or emotionally, you can send signals that can either encourage or discourage ideas. Some project managers can become so aggressive in their behavior that people simply tune out, while others are so low-key that they appear uncaring. As a project manager, you need to be aware of how your behavior is perceived so that you don't discourage idea generation and acceptance.

Ego. This includes you and everyone else. Emotional attachment to an idea may be strong. When an idea comes under attack, the impression may arise that the individual proposing the idea is under attack, too. It takes a strong character to separate one's own idea from one's ego. The fear of a bruised ego—not the rejection of one's idea—is enough to inhibit idea generation.

Tendency to act. Project managers favor action, due to the desire to see results quickly. Inquiry and analysis are viewed by many as not adding value and being too time consuming. A strong bias toward action can create an atmosphere of impatience with idea generation or at least thinking about the consequences of a poor idea. This attitude often results in rework and frustration, whereby the long-term cost of action exceeds the short-term cost of deliberation.

You will need to set the context to encourage creativity. This context should consist of

- Allowing time in the planning process for creative thought. Creativity cannot be manufactured on tap.
- Avoiding criticism of people but allowing critical thinking. Keep it from getting personal.
- Enabling opportunities for experimentation and risk taking. Recognize that failure is as normal as success.
- Encouraging cross-training, job enrichment, and job rotation. Provide people with the opportunities to learn from each other.
- Encouraging diversity of thought. Ask people to take different perspectives on issues.
- Encouraging the use of a wide array of creative thinking techniques. Train them on techniques such as brainstorming.
- Replenishing team membership with people having different backgrounds. New people often bring new ideas and varied perspectives.

As the context of the environment becomes conducive to idea generation, you will begin to collect them, either formally or informally. You will then have to determine which ones have merit.

First, apply some of the techniques discussed in this book to generate ideas, such as de Bono's Hat Thinking, brainstorming, and mind mapping. These approaches work well in offsetting idea inhibitors like groupthink, organizational culture, and mind guards.

Second, apply critical thinking. Encourage more questioning of assumptions; rely on facts and data to answer questions about an idea; generate multiple hypotheses about ideas and test validity; seek refutation as well as confirmation of an idea; follow the chain of logic of every idea, distinguishing between causes and correlations as well as distinguishing fact from fiction; and encourage debate over an idea in a way that elicits opposing ideas.

Third, minimize the emotion surrounding idea generation. Judged on their own merit, the previous two insights make complete sense. But even these approaches can be rendered useless when emotion takes over. The old sales idea that people buy on emotion and justify with facts is a constant threat when people attempt to generate and discuss an idea. Emotion can corrupt thinking on both individual and group levels.

Fourth, prepare to facilitate at team meetings to generate ideas. Some of your sessions may be earmarked for the specific purpose of generating ideas. You should, therefore, understand some basic principles of facilitation so that your sessions generate the necessary results.

A good facilitation session offers many benefits, including the opportunity to share information, build synergy, improve morale and esprit de corps, increase self-awareness among individuals and the entire team, and acquire a sense of empowerment. Realizing these benefits does not come easily, however.

Because you communicate 90% of your time, you are likely to share some of the following characteristics with facilitators: you are a good presenter, have a high tolerance for ambiguity, exhibit credibility and trustworthiness, and possess excellent problem-solving and conflict-management skills.

As a facilitator of a working session, you must ensure that all participants focus on attaining a common goal, such as fixing a problem. Hopefully, you will achieve consensus, resulting in all the participants leaving with a win-win feeling.

Preparation is key to having a successful facilitation session. This preparation includes having an agreed-upon agenda, a facility free of disturbances, a list of significant participants, a clear purpose, and identified roles for scribe and facilitator (if you are not the one), and a meeting leader.

Some additional keys to having a good facilitation session involve actual conduct. Ideally, the session should enable open dialogue, information sharing, empowerment of participants, an interruption-free environment, ownership of results, buy-in and commitment by all participants to group decisions, respect and tolerance for different opinions, synergy, and a positive, proactive atmosphere.

Follow-up is another key task for having a successful facilitation session. This follow-up entails having the scribe prepare and distribute the minutes and other related information. Another element of follow-up is obtaining feedback on items such as seeking additional information for preparing documents and implementing any changes.

With a good background in facilitation, you will need to have a corresponding knowledge of creative thinking tools and techniques. Some prevalent tools include brainstorming, mind mapping, de Bono Hat Thinking, critical thinking, and reflective thinking.

Brainstorming. This technique has been around for quite a while due to its popularity and ease of application. A group of people "blue-sky" ideas to address a problem. During the session, any idea is allowed to come forward; all evaluations and criticism are suspended until after recording all ideas; then they can evaluate ideas for their merit.

Some rules for effective brainstorming are

- "Piggy backing" on ideas: use an idea to generate another idea, and so on.
- Acting on results: encourage follow-up on the output of the brainstorming session.
- Asking open-ended, not closed or leading questions: allow people the freedom to expand on their thinking.
- Encouraging everyone to look "outside the box": have them step outside their paradigms.
- Keeping the membership of the session small, somewhere between seven and nine people: too many people can inhibit discussion.
- Limiting the duration of the session: time boxing encourages people to generate enough ideas within the time allotted.
- Loosening thinking to preclude people being locked into a paradigm: stop non-value-added criticism of ideas.
- Picking a scribe apart from the facilitator: capture results and encourage ownership.
- Trying to hold the session away from the work site: this action prevents interruptions.

Mind mapping. Another great technique to generate creative ideas on an individual level is to use mind mapping. This technique allows a person to generate ideas freely but at the same time capture their relationships among each other. Mind mapping, originated by Tony Buzan, exploits the neural net structure of the brain.

de Bono's Hat Thinking. Edward de Bono came up with a highly original and useful approach to applying different modes of thinking. The technique entails thinking of hats of different colors to wear when addressing a problem, for example. White-hat thinking is used to emphasize facts and data: red for emotion and intuition, black for negative perspective, yellow for positive perspective, green for idea generation, and blue for disciplined thinking.

Critical thinking. This category of thinking can be used with any technique for encouraging creativity on a project. It requires a disciplined approach that seeks to identify the fundamental assumptions, tenets, and facts—for example, of a theory or methodology. A key characteristic of critical thinking is asking the question "Why?"

Applied thinking. This is the other side of thinking. It requires applying the assumptions, tenets, and facts to achieve results. A key characteristic of applied thinking is asking the question:"How?"

Creativity requires both critical and applied thinking on projects. Asking "Why?" enables the determination of what has and has not worked well and whether what is occurring is adding value. Asking "How?" enables determining the necessary actions and then implementing them in a manner to effect change to achieve the vision of the project.

This activity is closely tied to the last one. In fact, the two activities can occur simultaneously. However, this activity will occur more smoothly if the "Why?" occurs first.

The premise behind this activity is that the people who do have the knowledge and experience know best how to improve it. You know what needs to happen; your team members know how to satisfy those needs. Oddly enough, this point is often overlooked by both project and functional managers.

There are two ways to solicit feedback on improving project performance. Each method can be used with the other.

The first approach is to meet with each person individually. This approach has many advantages. People tend to speak more frankly, they feel more relaxed, and you have an opportunity to probe for additional information. The downside of this approach is that some or all team members may be unwilling to share any insights.

Their reluctance may be due to mistrust. Some team members may have liked the previous project manager, they may feel you are a tool of the management, or they may believe you will not share credit for suggestions or recommendations. To instill trust, therefore, you should stress the importance of confidentiality and emphasize that people will receive credit for their recommendations and suggestions. Also, you should stress the confidentiality of one-on-one sessions.

An alternative is to have a group session with all the team members. You assemble everyone in a room, encourage suggestions and recommendations, and emphasize the need to keep an open mind.

This approach offers several advantages. It allows everyone to assemble as a team, thereby giving everyone an opportunity to know each other and to share experiences and knowledge. If conducted well, it can generate many useful suggestions and recommendations quickly and eliminate poor ones. It can also allow you to "piggy-back" on other suggestions to generate even better ones.

There are some disadvantages, too. People can become reticent, being fearful of retaliation or peer pressure. Suggestions and recommendations can be mocked by others, for example, thereby inhibiting generation of ideas. Disagreements can turn into divisiveness and recriminations, such as accusing other people of poor performance. It can also serve as a vehicle for people to showcase themselves, thus changing the focus of the session from improvement to self-promotion or posturing.

Ideally, the best approach is to apply one-on-one sessions and then follow up with a group session. For example, you can compile results of one-on-one sessions and present them to the team for assessment and feedback. You will then have a good idea of which suggestions and recommendations are useful and which ones are not. You will also receive good feedback regarding the risks and challenges surrounding each of the different suggestions and recommendations.

Regardless of the approach, team members should have a greater sense of ownership in the outcome of the project. Perhaps most importantly, you will have started building a dialogue with all team members.

When looking at the current schedule, you and your team should look for areas of improvement that make it more realistic, allow for more efficient execution, and enable the achievement of goals and objectives. To do that,

- After generating histograms for each resource, look for opportunities to level their profiles.
- Ascertain the degree of integration among tasks.
- Check the quality and quantity of resources.
- Consider technology as an opportunity to reduce labor requirements.
- Determine if touch points with other projects are affecting performance.
- Distinguish between hard and soft logic, and alter the latter to improve schedule performance.
- Don't employ too many concurrent, or parallel, tasks.
- Ensure that tasks are defined down to a meaningful level to serve as a tool for measuring progress.
- Ensure that anyone working on a task has given his or her concurrence to work on it.
- Evaluate the practicality of each constraint date.

- Look at resource allocation from an individual and group perspective.
- Check if there are too many burst-and-merge relationships among tasks, thereby increasing risks.
- Look for opportunities to crash the project.
- Verify that planning packages are being used; sometimes they are bypassed as an excuse for not planning in greater detail.
- Verify that all stakeholders, especially team members, understand their assignments.
- When reallocating resources, keep these guidelines in mind:
  - Give preference to tasks on the critical path.
- For concurrent tasks, give preference to the task with the most negative float or ones with the most complexity.

While reviewing resource allocation, look for areas of improvement. These improvements should focus on efficient and effective assignment of resources. To do that,

- Ensure sufficient lead time in the schedule to procure resources.
- For multiple labor resources on a task, ensure that one person is assigned responsibility for results.
- Identify assignments reflecting overallocations on the critical path.
- Look for tasks in the schedule that are sliding due to poor resource allocation.
- Pinpoint overallocation of resources on the critical path.
- Review past assignments and performance, paying particular attention to schedule slides.
- Verify that sufficient oversight over contractors is happening.

While reviewing budget performance, look for ways to reduce costs for labor, equipment, training, facilities, travel, information, and other resources needed to complete the project. Also, look at how the management and contingency reserves have been handled up to this point in time.

Additional factors to look for are whether

- Adequate oversight of costs by vendors and the project team have occurred.
- Compliance with managerial direction has occurred.
- Expenditures have adhered to organizational policies and procedures.

- Monies have been allocated, preferably to critical tasks.
- Original cost estimates were reasonable.
- Tracking cost and schedule performance are linked.
- Work authorization controls are in place to provide discipline in managing the budget.

While reviewing performance related to quality, look for ways to improve the quality of output. Look at

- Applicable quality standards
- Effectiveness of change management
- Level of quality sought, such as Three or Six Sigma
- Use and interpretation of quality control tools
- Value of existing metrics
- Whether gold plating is occurring
- Whether inspection is emphasized over prevention

While reviewing the management of procurements, look for opportunities to

- Avoid problems related to contract interpretation.
- Clarify roles and responsibilities between project stakeholders and vendors.
- Comply with government laws and regulations.
- Determine the most appropriate type of contract with the vendor.
- Improve the management of issues between project stakeholders and vendors.
- Minimize bureaucracy.
- Provide better oversight of vendors.
- Streamline procurement policies and procedures.

When looking at the effectiveness of communications, look for areas of improvement that encourage greater sharing of information and dialogue among stakeholders. To do that

- Ascertain whether stakeholders are receiving the right information at the right time in the right amount in the right format.
- Consider creating a repository of project information that enables people to gain the necessary access.

- Decide whether to set up a control room or war room and, if so, determine the purpose.
- Determine the reliability of existing documentation, such as procedures, policies, project manual, etc.
- Determine what data and information are necessary to maintain a reliable audit trail.
- Evaluate the value of information produced from reports; discontinue needless reporting.
- Evaluate the value of the data captured via hard or soft copy forms; remove collection of data that serves no value.
- Identify activities on the project that impede effective and efficient communications, and make the necessary changes.
- Look at how well the project has managed customer expectations.
- Review communications media to determine the compatibility and reliability.
- Review the communications plan, if one exists, to determine its accuracy and completeness.

When looking at the management of the scope, pay particular attention to how to maintain the integrity of the baselines for schedule, cost, and scope. To do that,

- Ascertain the value of existing change management metrics and determine the revisions, if necessary.
- Determine how the project evaluates the importance and impact of a change.
- Look at how the project obtains feedback or the effectiveness of a change.
- Pay particular attention to how well the project precludes scope creep or gold plating.
- Review all policies, procedures, and practices for analyzing, evaluating, and implementing changes to baselines.
- Review change management processes to ensure it has not become too bureaucratic or too light.
- Review configuration management tools and practices to identify opportunities for improvement.
- Review the approach to analyzing the impact of a change to cost, schedule, and scope baseline.

- Review the change control log, looking for completeness of entries and trends revealed in the data.
- Review the medium to collect data about changes.

When looking at risk management, look for ways to improve identification, analysis, and response. To do that,

- Ascertain the effectiveness of both risk responses, including strategies and contingencies, and follow up on the effectiveness of responses.
- Determine whether risk management is a one-time event or if it is conducted throughout the life cycle of the project.
- Determine whether risk owners have been assigned, and if so, how knowledgeable they are about their roles and responsibilities.
- Ensure that risk management is integrated with cost, schedule, and scope baselines.
- Evaluate the definitions used for likelihood, probability, and impact.
- Review the approach taken to qualitative and quantitative risk management.
- Review the effectiveness procedures and techniques used for risk identification, risk analysis, risk responses, risk monitoring, and risk reporting.
- Review the processes that maximize the impact of opportunities (positive risks) and minimize the impact of threats (negative threats).

When looking at the monitoring and controlling of schedule and cost performance, pay particular attention to the following baselines and know when to take remedial action. To do that,

- Act to improve cost and schedule performance when recovery planning has occurred; look at what was done in the past and determine the effectiveness of these actions.
- Ascertain the value of existing metrics on performance, and determine what additional ones are necessary and which current ones need to be changed or dropped.
- Evaluate the breadth and depth of controls on the project, looking at the necessity and adequacy of approvals, reviews, metrics, reporting, status collection and assessments, follow-up, organizational structure, etc.
- If using earned value, determine if people understand the calculated results and are using them.

- If using earned value, determine if the data used to generate calculated results is valid and if data is being collected consistently.
- Review processes and procedures for reviewing project performance and assessing how well the team is performing to plan.
- Review the effectiveness of recovery actions for corrective actions and replanning.
- Review the efficiency and effectiveness of current processes and procedures for collecting and analyzing cost and schedule status.

4.5 3.4: REMOVE THE NON-VALUE-ADDED WORK

This activity, which is closely allied to the previous activity, seeks to remove any materials, machines, methods, or resources that do not contribute directly toward achieving the goals and objectives of your project. You and your team members should stop or suspend anything not contributing to the vision to avoid wasting energy and effort.

Similar to earlier efforts by the core team, team members should use the new or revised charter or statement of work to determine what to suspend or stop. A solid understanding of the scope or boundaries is very useful in determining which activities add value and which ones do not.

Applying a systems perspective will also help. The benefit of this perspective is that it enables team members to see the big picture and, more importantly, how they contribute to the vision. Armed with this information, they may find that what they do fails to contribute to achieving the overall goals and objectives. Or, they may discover how to improve their contribution to the overall success of the project. Of course, they may also see that they are already significantly contributing to a successful outcome.

Naturally, you may find it necessary to call another time-out before obtaining feedback. People are often busy doing their work and do not think about priorities from a big-picture perspective. Or, they may view anything other than not performing "hands-on" work as a waste of time. Nevertheless, it's best to hold discussions in a place separate from the work area, such as a conference room or the company cafeteria, to preclude interruptions and other influences.

Removing non-value-added activities offers the same benefits described earlier in the case of the core team. It enables team members to focus on what matters, lays the groundwork for a higher level of performance, and obtains buy-in for changes being implemented. Particularly useful here is applying the principles of Lean that were described earlier.

A lessons learned session, too, will prove useful not just for generating options but also for identifying non-value-added tasks. One of the most important actions that you can take as a project manager when taking over a project in trouble is to learn about what occurred in the past, and conducting a lessons learned session is the way to achieve that.

Conducting a lessons learned session, however, can pose some challenges, especially for a project in trouble. The reasons are many. Some people may harbor emotional baggage. The desire to point fingers will surface in overt and subtle ways. Negative conflict at the session can potentially turn explosive. Some people will see you as using the session to remove certain individuals.

You can meet with people individually or as a group, or both. Regardless of the approach, don't lose this opportunity to learn from the past; it will give you clues on how to turn around the project. It will, if conducted well, increase commitment to the project, especially if feedback results in substantive changes.

A lessons learned session should address several topics. These topics include what went well; what areas need improvement; what tools, techniques, and practices could be applied differently; and what to leverage from the past for future projects.

4.6 3.5: IDENTIFY OPTIONS

After completing all the processes and their corresponding activities up to this point in time, you, in concert with your team, should have enough facts and data to generate options to improve performance. You have looked at past performance, interviewed team members and other stakeholders, and identified and implemented a new or revised charter and statement of work or both. You are now ready to identify options to improve performance.

There are three caveats that you and your team should consider when identifying options.

First, keep an open mind. A tendency exists to allow one's prejudices— for example, values, beliefs, norms, and assumptions—to take over and influence the identification of options. Peer pressure can also have a profound, and subtle, influence. When prejudices take over, options are quickly eliminated, for example, that may actually be more efficient and effective than the ones eventually listed, or adjusted in such a way as to reduce their effectiveness. Strong personalities are often the cause for this situation, leading frequently to popular solutions but not necessarily effective ones.

Second, avoid jumping to a solution before defining the problem or issue. A tendency exists, particularly in Western cultures, to come up with a solution before carefully defining the problem. This approach is riddled with many problems despite offering a quick fix. It can "force" a solution that may provide relief for the moment but introduce severe consequences later during the project life cycle. Individuals who must implement the solution may react negatively. Finally, the solution might not work correctly from the outset, resulting in a cost of rework or effort that exceeds the cost of not addressing the problem; that is, the costs of the solution exceed the benefits.

By taking the time to identify solutions, or options, based on feedback, you and your core team can realize three benefits.

The first benefit is that by enumerating options, you now have the flexibility to determine the best option to deal with a problem, issue, or shortcoming. You can become eclectic by selecting the most appropriate option or options after the next process—4.0: Evaluate.

The second benefit is that it helps maintain objectivity. A listing of options will prevent you and core team members from caving in to prejudices. The act of building a list of options forces people to consider other ideas. Making this list more visible may encourage discussion over options and encourage looking at the pros and cons of each option.

The third benefit is that it is a good way to remove negative emotion. Identifying and discussing options discourages people from harboring resentments over why an option was selected and complaining that they had no opportunity to provide feedback. The eventual selection of an option appears less arbitrary and capricious to the individuals implementing it.

The more options, the better. Generating options for eventual evaluation, unfortunately, does not come easily. You have to work at generating them and, fortunately, there is a wide range of tools and techniques for doing just that. What follows is a description of some of the common tools and techniques used for generating options using either an individual or group approach.

Ishikawa diagram. More commonly known as the fishbone diagram, this approach requires defining a problem and then identifying the causes, usually from a manpower, machine, methods, and material perspective, though you can use some other categories to replace or supplement the four just mentioned.

After completing the diagram and performing the necessary analysis, you and your team can then develop a list of options for fixing the problem. Defining the problem clearly and identifying the causes enables you and your team to develop a specific set of options for eventual evaluation.

Lessons learned. This approach, often generated at the conclusion of a phase, major milestone, or project, is used to capture what went well and what areas needed improvement. The description of what went well during a previous phase or milestone accomplishment may provide some options for addressing current problems. Areas identified as needing improvement offer ideas that can be used to develop options. Of course, lessons learned documents from previous projects of a similar nature may provide a rich source of ideas for options to consider.

Brainstorming. Already discussed previously, this approach can also be used to generate options for eventual evaluation. The key is to avoid making judgments during the session. A good point to remember when generating options during brainstorming sessions is to "piggy-back" from one option to another to generate a series of related options.

Interviewing. You can meet with subject matter experts (SMEs) or key stakeholders to generate options to conduct an interview. Sometimes, interviewing people who do not have a vested interest in your project is an excellent way to generate options.

You can pursue a structured or unstructured interview or a blend of both. A structured interview provides a set of prefabricated questions; an unstructured interview involves spontaneous questions. The unstructured approach provides the opportunity to generate options because it allows both the interviewer and interviewee the capability to explore ideas that might be ignored using a structured approach. In other words, it allows both parties to think outside the box, possibly leading to options that would never have arisen during a structured interview session.

Benchmarking. This approach may generate options because it requires comparing current processes, procedures, and practices with those of other organizations or projects. Variances identified in the comparison may provide insights into what areas to improve upon and generate ideas for options. This approach helps you and your team open new horizons for generating options.

Nominal group technique. Frequently referred to as NGT, this approach is a derivative of brainstorming. The specific differences are that the generated lists of ideas or options are combined or categorized and others are eliminated. Then—and this applies more to the selected options—a vote is taken to select the best options. As with brainstorming in its pure form, you and your team need to avoid judgment until option generation is complete, after which combining, eliminating, and selecting can occur.

Mind mapping. As mentioned in another part of this book, mind mapping is a tool for identifying the components of a concept and then identifying the relationships among them. The relationships are nonhierarchical, similar to a neural network. It is an excellent tool for performing individual brainstorming of coming up with options and then identifying the relationships among them.

Modeling. Developing models, such as diagrams, about a process, procedure, or practice, is a good way to understand the status quo; it is also a useful way to generate options. As you sit with your team, the very act of building a model will raise questions and ideas related to improving project performance. Not only will you and your team identify components but also the relationships among those components, thereby identifying opportunities to combine, change, remove, automate, etc. By developing and reviewing a model, the fundamental question of "Why?" needs to be asked repeatedly.

A good model, if it is to be useful for generating options, should have two key characteristics. It should reflect reality as closely as possible. It should also be understandable by the people referring to it. Some examples of models include data flow diagrams, object-oriented diagrams, flowcharts, hierarchy charts, influence diagrams, and many more.

Literature review. In today's information-rich environment, the challenge is not so much getting information but finding the information you need. There are plenty of journals, Web sites, books, and magazines that give you more information than you likely need or want. Popular in trade journals are articles about experiences in their particular niche; sometimes, however, reading journals for your project that are outside your field can provide insight as to options that no one ever thought about.

Different perspectives. Related to the last point but in a broader sense is the fact that a search for different perspectives on a problem may reveal information that will enable you and your team to generate options that no one could ever have thought about. In the age of specialization, there is a strong tendency for people to become so specialized that it becomes almost impossible to think outside the box; few renaissance thinkers exist today. Ways to broaden perspectives include reading material that challenges accepted viewpoints, interviewing people in different fields and industries, role playing, and attending conferences that people from different fields attend.

Visualization. A good way to determine options is to visualize in your mind's eye what you and your team consider the perfect state of affairs. Using that visualization, compare that idealized state with reality. The differences may give you and your team some options to consider. A good technique is to capture the visualization and the existing situation on paper and then compare the two, noting the differences. These differences will help develop options. This approach is also known as *imagineering*.

Analogies, metaphors, and similes. You and your team can take a more "literary" approach to developing options by using analogies, metaphors, and similes by comparing the project to something that is either similar or dissimilar, and then taking that information to derive some useful options. This approach can be used with brainstorming techniques.

Free association. Closely related to the last approach discussed, this technique tries to achieve a mental connection between two concepts or items. You can simply describe a problem or situation, identify a word or thought that you associate with it, and then expand the relationship to develop some options to address the problem. Hence, the sequence is problem, word, or thought, and then options. Under free association, the problem and the word or thought do not have to be related directly; under regular association, they do.

Synectics. This approach makes use of analogies to generate options to solve problems and come up with a recommendation. The leader of the group states a problem and then the group restates it, followed by the picking of the best one by the customer. Next, the group develops options and cites strengths and weaknesses for each one. Within a specified period of time, the group comes up with a proposed solution, or selected option.

SWOT analysis. The acronym stands for Strengths, Weaknesses, Opportunities, and Threats. You or your team or both brainstorm a series of options. Then, for each option, you and your team identify the aspects of the option that enable the achievement of project objectives (strengths), shortcomings that can impede the achievement of objectives (weaknesses), opportunities (conditions that further their achievement), and threats

Option	Strengths	Weaknesses	Opportunities	Threats

FIGURE 4.3
SWOT table.

(conditions that threaten their achievement). Figure 4.3 shows a table commonly used for SWOT analysis.

Cause and effect graph. Like the fishbone diagram, this graph is a good way to identify the causes of problems and then generate options. What makes this graph different from the fishbone diagram is that a series of bubbles are drawn to show the relationship between causes, intermediate causes, and effects. After drawing and reviewing the charts, you can then develop a series of options that remove the source of the problem. Below is an example of a cause and effect graph.

Chunking and affinitizing. This approach, often associated with analysis, is taking an idea, problem, or object, and then breaking it down into manageable pieces according to some criteria. Ideally, the criteria are based on some natural divisions. The size and depth of chunking depends on what heuristics, or rules of thumb, you are using. After chunking the idea or object, you can then regroup the parts according to some criteria. You can use both chunking and affinitizing to generate options to solve a particular problem. Sometimes, breaking down something into its constituent parts and recombining them enables you to discover something that you would ordinarily not discover, in this case, one or more options.

Crawford slip technique. This technique derives from brainstorming. It gives a group of people a short time to generate ideas on note cards to address a well-defined problem statement. Participants then go through the cards and affinitize them, or put them into categories. After a while, not only does the number of ideas get whittled down but so does the number of categories. Then a final report is provided to everyone on the results.

The Crawford slip technique is a way to identify groups of options that you can eventually evaluate.

Storyboarding. This technique is also a derivative of brainstorming options; you can use it to turn around your project. It goes beyond merely identifying options; it also helps in identifying their interrelationships.

Like all the other techniques, this one requires clearly defining the problem up front. Armed with a good definition, the group of people assigned to address the problem divides the problem statement into different topics. The group then generates issues and solutions to each of the topics, both at the strategic and operational levels.

The next set of steps is to generate storyboards addressing four different areas: planning, ideas, organization, and communications. These are essentially ways to expand on the options generated earlier and provide a game plan for their implementation by answering the what, who, when, where, why, and how. Each storyboard consists of two sessions: creative and critical. The former generates ideas, and the latter critiques them. Though storyboarding works, it can become quite complicated and time consuming. Still, it is yet another effective way to generate options.

Here are some typical options for improving schedule performance:

- Stop vacations and training.
- Concentrate only on critical tasks.
- Crash the schedule.
- Employ phased implementation.
- Employ positive and negative incentives.
- Employ shift work.
- Fast-track the schedule.
- Hire more competent people.
- Improve communications.
- Lower quality.
- Outsource.
- Purchase better equipment and tools.
- Rebaseline for cost and schedule.
- Reduce scope.
- Streamline processes; for example, reduce the number of reviews.
- Upgrade skill levels.
- Work overtime.

Here are some typical options to improve cost performance:

- Acquire a system or tool and eliminate the need for labor.
- Execute only processes and procedures that add value to the final product.
- Focus only on critical tasks.
- Hire cheaper labor.
- Improve communications.
- Outsource.
- Reduce cycle time.
- Reduce incentives.
- Reduce or eliminate overtime.
- Reduce or eliminate training.
- Reduce scope.
- Reduce team size.
- Streamline processes.
- Use less equipment and supplies.

Here are some typical options to improve quality performance:

- Acquire better tools and equipment.
- Conduct assessments and self-audits.
- Encourage cross-checking.
- Hire only qualified people.
- Improve communications.
- Increase performance standards.
- Increase training and knowledge sharing.
- Institute quality control measures.
- Institute rigorous change control and configuration management.

Here are some typical options to improve communications:

- Adopt new technology, such as social network software, Wiki, blogs, portal, and project mapping tools.
- Create a set of meaningful forms to collect data.
- Create a standard set of reports.
- Establish a project library.
- Establish a project repository.
- Start a project management office.
- Identify formats for memoranda and e-mails.
- Identify key meetings, for example, status review.

- Prepare a new or revised communications plan.
- Prepare a standard agenda for standard meetings, for example, checkpoint (gate) review.
- Prepare common project processes and procedures.
- Provide a project manual for all team members and other key stakeholders.
- Publish a newsletter.
- Set up a control, or war, room.
- Set up project history files.

Here are some typical options to improve human resource management:

- Clarify roles and responsibilities.
- Create an organization chart.
- Encourage creativity.
- Establish both positive rewards and negative incentives.
- Increase cross-training.
- Increase empowerment.
- Increase job enlargement.
- Increase job enrichment.
- Increase team participation.
- Obtain greater stakeholder involvement.
- Perform resource leveling.
- Plan celebrations at key milestone dates.
- Prepare a responsibility assignment matrix.
- Reduce burnout.
- Reduce excessive overtime.
- Reduce fear.
- Reduce frustration.
- Reduce negative conflict.
- Reduce negativism.
- Reduce procrastination.
- Revise team structure.

Here are some typical options to improve procurement management:

- Establish a dispute resolution process.
- Establish guidelines on working with consultants.
- Establish guidelines on working with contractors.

- Establish guidelines on working with suppliers.
- Modify existing contract types, for example, fixed price.
- Revise approaches toward vendor selection.
- Set up a process with vendors for receiving performance status.
- Set up a review for statements of work.
- Set up a review process for requests for proposals.
- Verify compliance with existing contracts.

Here are some options to improve scope management:

- Apply configuration management.
- Control scope creep.
- Create a change request form.
- Create a change request log.
- Define impacts.
- Define probability or likelihood.
- Determine metrics to track changes.
- Develop formal change control processes and procedures.
- Establish a change board.
- Identify categories of change.
- Identify priorities of change.
- Purchase a configuration management tool.

Here are some typical options to improve risk management practices:

- Adjust schedule and costs to reflect the impact of identified risks.
- Build a risk breakdown structure.
- Define risk impact.
- Define risk likelihood or probability.
- Determine when to perform qualitative risk analysis.
- Determine when to perform quantitative risk analysis.
- Develop a risk matrix.
- Establish a process for reporting on risks and risk responses.
- Establish a risk management log.
- Establish an approach to analyzing risks.
- Establish an approach to identifying risks.
- Establish an approach to monitoring effectiveness of risk responses.
- Establish an approach to responding to risks.
- Identify risk owners.

- Identify risks.
- Identify sources of data to perform risk management.
- Make adjustments to contingency reserves.
- Make adjustments to management reserves.

Here are some typical options to improve project execution:

- Adjust performance standards.
- Apply a problem-solving approach.
- Concentrate on the critical path.
- Control out-of-scope tasks.
- Deploy change management.
- Focus on key milestone dates.
- Focus on the vision.
- Follow a standardized process.
- Follow cost and schedule plans.
- Identify metrics on cost, schedule, and quality performance.
- Increase training.
- Maintain baselines.
- Manage customer expectations.
- Outsource work.
- Postpone or cancel tasks not adding value.
- Purchase components.
- Purchase tools to enhance performance.
- Redistribute workload among resources.
- Reuse previous work.
- Set priority among cost, schedule, and quality.
- Track output with requirements.
- Work with key stakeholders.

Here are some typical options to improve monitoring and controlling:

- Define key variances requiring attention.
- Determine data and information to monitor cost and schedule performance.
- Determine data and information to track past cost and schedule performance.
- Determine key actions to perform recovery planning, for example, corrective action, replanning.

- Determine key considerations for status collection, for example, reporting period, time units, rates.
- Determine meetings and set up standardized agendas.
- Determine necessary project controls.
- Establish earned value management.
- Establish gate reviews.
- Establish processes and procedures for collecting status.
- Obtain the best tool to collect and compile progress data.
- Tailor reports to the needs of stakeholders.

Though many of the above options will work, there are some projects, perhaps yours, that pose some special challenges that may require some additional considerations for options.

Globalization. If you take over this type of project, the likelihood is high that some problems will arise due to differences in language, culture, time zones, laws, currency, and procedures. These variables often introduce serious risks in a project and, if left unattended, could become issues that are difficult to rectify. Some ways to address these challenges are to sensitize team members to such differences and then provide opportunities to address them as best as possible. Regular ongoing communications, diversity training, and collaboration among team members from different countries on tasks are good ways to help turn around a globalization project in trouble.

Virtual teams. With the rise of information technology (IT) as a tool of production and with the cost of travel increasing, virtual teams have become more common. The challenges are innumerable, however. Some of them include differences in communication style, for example, some prefer face-to-face meetings rather than the electronic medium to communicate; technological incompatibility, for example, different protocols; vast differences in time zones; difficulty in providing oversight of performance; and team-building challenges, for example, cultural preferences reflecting a desire to work alone rather than in a group. Ongoing communications, common processes, and clear responsibilities, accountabilities, and authorities are ways to improve the performance of virtual teams.

Outsourcing. Similar to virtual teams, outsourcing has become prevalent, especially in the IT arena. While it may offer many advantages, it also presents some serious challenges. A project employing outsourcing to produce deliverables presents challenges such as the seller and the buyer having differences in procedures and culture, operating in different time zones, employing incompatible technologies, and the latter resisting oversight by the former on performance. These challenges can seriously strain the relations between both parties. If your project outsources some deliverables, consider engaging members from the vendor to attend your project meetings; establish regular performance reporting; institute common processes, procedures, and practices; and use compatible tools.

Compliance. In recent years, compliance projects and projects impacted by regulatory requirements have become more commonplace, and this trend is likely to continue. Issues related to ethics, overhead for oversight, differences between governmental institutions, and the fear of being held accountable for failure to comply have a big influence on the performance of these projects. If your project is in trouble due to compliance or regulatory issues, consider instituting gate reviews that require legal review of deliverables prior to moving to the next phase, reducing the number of approvals by consolidating them, and having stakeholders sign statements attesting that there is no risk of compliance violations, for example, conflicts of interest, on account of their participation on the project.

4.7 CONCLUSION

One of the biggest dangers of recovering a project in trouble is the failure to maintain objectivity. There is a tendency for a new project manager and the core team members to become arrogant and not consider the suggestions, ideas, opinions, etc. of other stakeholders. Quite often, team members are not viewed as stakeholders and, therefore, have nothing to contribute. By obtaining input, a project manager not only generates a solid list of options but also lays the groundwork for support to execute effective change.

Case Study (*Continued*)

Explore. After the first session, Deborah thought the next step was to have an open discussion about their thoughts. The visioning session, as she called it, had facilitated effective communications among team members. Such communications had never occurred before; Harold, the system architect, decided to boycott this meeting too, an act that did not please the manager, Fred. However, Harold's absence enabled the team to engage in open communications for the first time. Team members expressed themselves even more fully about what they wanted to see on the project. The exchange of feelings and information flowed like never before; even some of the team members started expressing a greater interest on working on some of the components of the system.

While reviewing the diagram from a systemic perspective, Deborah asked the core team to determine where the biggest problems occurred, both from the product and process perspectives. She asked them to see if they could come up with ideas on how to improve processes as well as features and functionalities of the final deliverable. She was particularly interested in looking at ways of removing non-value-added work as they related to data, tools, people, and processes. It was decided that the team needed an important upgrade to the software tool and that everyone on the team was lacking a way to back up their work. Several times in the past, developers' laptops, for example, had failed and because they did not back up their work, they had to redo it. The team also suggested that they develop programming standards so that team members could communicate. Finally, some team members found out that they were duplicating the work of others and that some were waiting for work to be completed that had, unknown to them, already been completed.

Once the team felt comfortable expressing their concerns and feelings, and sharing information about the past and the present, Deborah had the team identify options for improving the project. These options included managerial as well as technical topics. Some of the options included taking a more incremental approach toward delivery of the product, purchasing components for the application rather than building them, outsourcing other components to be built, using prototyping to capture requirements, building a data model for the application, and implementing some project management disciplines, including building an integrated schedule and implementing change management.

4.8 GETTING-STARTED CHECKLIST

Question	Yes	No
1. Have you decided to conduct a lessons learned session?	____	____
If yes, will the lessons learned address the following topics:	____	____
What went well?	____	____
What areas need improvement?	____	____
What tools, techniques, and practices could be applied differently?	____	____
What can be leveraged from the past for the next project?	____	____
2. Do you get people to share feelings and information by		
Holding one-on-one sessions with individual team members?	____	____
Holding group sessions?	____	____
Holding a combination of individual and group sessions?	____	____
3. If communications are poor, have you identified any reasons like		
Management does not value nor want upward communications?	____	____
Fear of retaliation?	____	____
Fear of being humiliated?	____	____
Fear of being wrong?	____	____
Fear of being fired?	____	____
Fear of being a scapegoat?	____	____
4. To be an effective listener, do you		
Not interrupt, except to clarify a point?	____	____
Maintain eye contact?	____	____
Focus on the message?	____	____
Avoid preoccupations?	____	____
Stay on topic?	____	____
Empathize, not sympathize?	____	____
Watch body language?	____	____
5. Do you have a good understanding of the communications process?	____	____
6. To reduce the "noise" in communications, do you		
Recognize that noise exists and account for it when listening to the stakeholder?	____	____
Ask questions to uncover the cause of a problem, not just the symptoms?	____	____
Segregate facts and data from assumptions and opinions?	____	____
Consider alternative points of view?	____	____
Seek positive disagreement, not negative conflict, to bring out useful insights and information?	____	____
Look for alternative viewpoints to get a different perspective?	____	____
7. Do you recognize that everyone's interests are important?	____	____
8. Do you get people to think about the project's state and suggest improvements?	____	____

Question	Yes	No
9. Do you set the context for creativity by		
Encouraging diversity of thought?	___	___
Allowing time in the process for creative thought?	___	___
Encouraging a wide array of creative thinking technologies?	___	___
Avoiding criticism of people but allowing critical thinking about ideas?	___	___
Enabling opportunities for experimenting and risk taking?	___	___
Replenishing team membership with people with different backgrounds?	___	___
Encourage cross-training, job enrichment, and job rotation among team members?	___	___
10. For each facilitation session, is there		
Open dialogue?	___	___
Information sharing?	___	___
Empowerment of participants?	___	___
Ownership of results?	___	___
Buy-in and commitment by participants?	___	___
Respect and tolerance for different opinions?	___	___
A positive, proactive attitude?	___	___
Follow-up on results?	___	___
11. To encourage creativity during facilitation and working sessions, do you consider using		
Brainstorming?	___	___
Mind mapping?	___	___
de Bono's Hat Thinking?	___	___
Critical thinking?	___	___
Applied thinking?	___	___
12. Do you use technology to reduce labor requirements?	___	___
13. While reviewing resource allocation, do you		
Review past assignments and performance, paying particular attention to schedule slides?	___	___
Identify assignments reflecting overallocations on the critical path?	___	___
Pinpoint overallocation of resources on the critical path?	___	___
Look for tasks in the schedule that are sliding due to poor resource allocation?	___	___
For multiple labor resource on a task, ensure that one person is assigned responsibility for results?	___	___
Ensure that sufficient lead time is built into the schedule to procure resources?	___	___
Verify that sufficient oversight is happening over contractors?	___	___
14. While reviewing budget performance, do you look for opportunities to reduce costs for		

Question	Yes	No
Labor?	___	___
Equipment?	___	___
Training?	___	___
Facilities?	___	___
Travel?	___	___
Information?	___	___
15. Do you also look at how		
Management and contingency reserves have been handled up to this point in time?	___	___
Tracking cost and schedule performance are linked?	___	___
Work authorization controls are in place to ensure discipline in managing the budget?	___	___
Good compliance with managerial direction has been?	___	___
Expenditures have adhered to organizational policies and procedures?	___	___
Adequate oversight of costs by vendors and the project team have occurred?	___	___
Original cost estimates could have had a reasonable chance of being met?	___	___
Monies have been allocated, preferably to critical tasks?	___	___
16. While reviewing performance related to quality, do you look for ways to improve quality by looking at		
The applicable quality standards?	___	___
Whether gold plating is occurring?	___	___
Whether inspection is emphasized over prevention?	___	___
The value of existing metrics?	___	___
The use and interpretation of quality control tools?	___	___
The level of quality sought, such as Three or Six Sigma?	___	___
The effectiveness of change management?	___	___
17. While reviewing the management of procurements, do you look for opportunities to		
Minimize bureaucracy?	___	___
Streamline procurement policies and procedures?	___	___
Comply with government laws and regulations?	___	___
Provide better oversight of vendors?	___	___
Clarify roles and responsibilities between project stakeholders and vendors?	___	___
Avoid problems related to contract interpretation?	___	___
Improve the management of issues between project stakeholders and vendors?	___	___
Determine the most appropriate type of contract with the vendor?	___	___

Question	Yes	No
18. When looking at how well communications are going on your project, do you		
Review the communications plan, if one exists, to determine its accuracy and completeness?	____	____
Ascertain whether stakeholders are receiving the right information at the right time in the right amount in the right format?	____	____
Create a repository of project information that enables people to gain the necessary access?	____	____
Determine the reliability of existing documentation, such as procedures, policies, project manual, etc.?	____	____
Decide whether to set up a control room or war room and, if so, determine the purpose?	____	____
Review communications media to determine compatibility and reliability?	____	____
Evaluate the value of the data that is captured via hard or soft copy forms; remove collection of data that serves no value?	____	____
Evaluate the value of information that is produced from reports; discontinue needless reporting?	____	____
Determine what data and information are necessary to maintain a reliable audit trail?	____	____
Identify activities on the project that impede effective and efficient communications and make the necessary changes?	____	____
Look at how well the project has managed customer expectations?	____	____
19. When looking at how well the scope of the project is being managed, do you		
Review all policies, procedures, and practices for analyzing, evaluating, and implementing changes to baselines?	____	____
Pay particular attention to how well the project precludes scope creep or gold plating?	____	____
Determine how the project evaluates the importance and impact of a change?	____	____
Review the approach to analyzing the impact of a change to cost, schedule, and scope baseline?	____	____
Look at how the project obtains feedback on the effectiveness of a change?	____	____
Review change management processes to ensure they have not become too bureaucratic or too light?	____	____
Ascertain the value of existing change management metrics and determine the revisions, if necessary?	____	____
Review the change control log, looking for completeness of entries and trends revealed in the data?	____	____
Review the medium for collecting data about a change?	____	____

Question	Yes	No
Review configuration management tools and practices to identify opportunities for improvement?	___	___
20. When looking at risk management, do you		
Review the processes that maximize the impact of opportunities (positive risks) and minimize the impact of threats (negative threats)?	___	___
Evaluate the definitions used for likelihood, probability, and impact?	___	___
Review the approach taken for qualitative and quantitative risk management?	___	___
Ascertain the effectiveness of both risk responses, including strategies and contingencies, and follow up on the effectiveness of responses?	___	___
Determine whether they assign risk owners and, if so, how knowledgeable they are about their roles and responsibilities?	___	___
Review the effectiveness of procedures and techniques used for risk identification, risk analysis, risk responses, risk monitoring, and risk reporting?	___	___
Determine whether risk management is a one-time event or is conducted throughout the life cycle of the project?	___	___
Ensure that risk management is integrated with cost, schedule, and scope baselines?	___	___
21. When looking at the monitoring and controlling of schedule and cost performance, do you		
Review processes and procedures for reviewing project performance and assessing how the team is performing to plan?	___	___
Evaluate the breadth and depth of controls on the project, looking at the necessity and adequacy of approvals, reviews, metrics, reporting, status collection and assessments, follow-up, organizational structure, etc.?	___	___
Review the efficiency and effectiveness of current processes and procedures for collecting and analyzing cost and schedule status?	___	___
Ascertain the value of existing metrics on performance and determining which additional ones are necessary and which ones need changing or need to be dropped?	___	___
If using earned value, determine if the data used to generate calculated results is valid and that data is being collected consistently?	___	___
If using earned value, determine if people understand the calculated results and using them?	___	___
Act to improve cost and schedule performance when recovery planning has occurred, looking at what was done in the past and determining the effectiveness of these actions?	___	___

Question	Yes	No
Review the effectiveness of recovery actions for corrective actions and replanning?	___	___
22. When removing non-value-added items, do you		
Refer to the new or revised charter or statement of work?	___	___
Apply a systems perspective?	___	___
Ask for feedback on ideas?	___	___
Refer to the business case?	___	___
23. When identifying options, do you		
Keep an open mind?	___	___
Avoid jumping to the solutions before defining the problem area or issue?	___	___
24. Do you consider the following options for improving schedule performance:		
Rebaselining?	___	___
Hiring more competent people?	___	___
Purchasing better equipment and tools?	___	___
Streamlining processes, for example, reducing the number of reviews?	___	___
Lowering quality?	___	___
Reducing scope?	___	___
Employing phased implementation?	___	___
Outsourcing?	___	___
Concentrating only on critical tasks?	___	___
Working overtime?	___	___
Employing shift work?	___	___
Ceasing vacations and training?	___	___
Employing positive and negative incentives?	___	___
Upgrading skills levels?	___	___
Improving communications?	___	___
Fast-tracking the schedule?	___	___
Crashing the schedule?	___	___
25. Do you consider the following options for improving cost performance:		
Reducing scope?	___	___
Reducing team size?	___	___
Hiring cheap labor?	___	___
Using less equipment and supplies?	___	___
Streamlining processes?	___	___
Reducing or eliminating training?	___	___
Reducing or eliminating overtime?	___	___
Reducing incentives?	___	___
Improving communications?	___	___

Question	Yes	No
Outsourcing?	___	___
Reducing cycle time?	___	___
Executing processes and procedures only adding value to the final product?	___	___
Acquiring a system or tool, eliminating the need for labor?	___	___
Focusing only on critical tasks?	___	___
26. Do you consider the following options for improving quality performance:		
Increasing performance standards?	___	___
Instituting rigorous change control and configuration management?	___	___
Hiring only qualified people?	___	___
Conducting assessments and self-audits?	___	___
Instituting quality control measures?	___	___
Encouraging cross-checking?	___	___
Increasing training and knowledge sharing?	___	___
Acquiring better tools and equipment?	___	___
Improving communications?	___	___
27. Do you consider the following options for improving communications:		
Preparing a new or revised communications plan?	___	___
Establishing a project repository?	___	___
Establishing a project library?	___	___
Setting up project history files?	___	___
Providing a project manual to all team members and other key stakeholders?	___	___
Preparing common project processes and procedures?	___	___
Forming a project management office?	___	___
Creating a set of meaningful forms to collect data?	___	___
Creating a standard set of reports?	___	___
Identifying formats for memorandum and e-mails?	___	___
Publishing a newsletter?	___	___
Identifying key meetings, for example, status review?	___	___
Preparing a standard agenda for standard meetings, for example, checkpoint (gate) review?	___	___
Setting up a control room or war room?	___	___
Adopting new technology, such as social network software, Wiki, blog, portal, and project mapping tools?	___	___
28. Do you consider the following options for improving human resource management:		
Establishing both positive rewards and negative incentives?	___	___
Planning celebrations at key milestone dates?	___	___
Reducing frustration?	___	___

Question	Yes	No
Reducing procrastination?	___	___
Reducing fear?	___	___
Reducing excessive overtime?	___	___
Reducing burnout?	___	___
Reducing negative conflict?	___	___
Increasing team participation?	___	___
Reducing negativism?	___	___
Increasing cross-training?	___	___
Increasing job enrichment?	___	___
Increasing job enlargement?	___	___
Increasing empowerment?	___	___
Encouraging creativity?	___	___
Obtaining greater stakeholder involvement?	___	___
Performing resource leveling?	___	___
Preparing a responsibility matrix?	___	___
Clarifying roles and responsibilities?	___	___
Creating an organization chart?	___	___
Revising team structure?	___	___
29. Do you consider the following options for improving procurement management:		
Modifying existing contract types?	___	___
Revising approaches toward selecting vendors?	___	___
Verifying compliance with existing contracts?	___	___
Establishing a dispute resolution process?	___	___
Setting up a review process for requests for proposals?	___	___
Setting up a review process for statements of work?	___	___
Establishing guidelines on working with suppliers?	___	___
Establishing guidelines on working with contractors?	___	___
Establishing guidelines on working with consultants?	___	___
Setting up a process for receiving performance status with vendors?	___	___
30. Do you consider the following options for improving scope management:		
Defining impacts?	___	___
Defining probability or likelihood?	___	___
Developing formal change control processes and procedures?	___	___
Identifying priorities of change?	___	___
Identifying categories of change?	___	___
Controlling scope creep?	___	___
Establishing a change board?	___	___
Creating a change request form?	___	___
Applying configuration management?	___	___

Question	Yes	No
Purchasing configuration management tools?	___	___
Determining metrics to track changes?	___	___
31. Do you consider the following options for improving risk management practices:		
Identifying sources of data to perform risk management?	___	___
Identifying risk owners?	___	___
Identifying risks?	___	___
Defining risk or likelihood?	___	___
Defining risk impact?	___	___
Establishing an approach for identifying risks?	___	___
Establishing an approach for analyzing risks?	___	___
Establishing an approach for responding to risks?	___	___
Establishing an approach for monitoring effectiveness of risk responses?	___	___
Establishing a process for reporting on risks and risk responses?	___	___
Building a risk breakdown structure?	___	___
Determining when to perform qualitative risk analysis?	___	___
Determining when to perform quantitative risk analysis?	___	___
Developing a risk matrix?	___	___
Establishing a risk management log?	___	___
Adjusting schedule and costs to reflect impact of identified risks?	___	___
Making adjustments to contingency reserves?	___	___
Making adjustments to management reserves?	___	___
32. Do you consider the following options for improving project execution:		
Setting priority among cost, schedule, and quality?	___	___
Redistributing the workload among resources?	___	___
Concentrating on the critical path?	___	___
Managing customer expectations?	___	___
Controlling out-of-scope tasks?	___	___
Tracking output with requirements?	___	___
Maintaining baselines?	___	___
Identifying metrics on cost, schedule, and quality performance?	___	___
Focusing on the vision?	___	___
Following cost and schedule plans?	___	___
Deploying change management?	___	___
Applying a problem-solving approach?	___	___
Following a standardized process?	___	___
Reusing previous work?	___	___
Postponing or canceling tasks not adding value?	___	___
Purchasing components?	___	___

Question	Yes	No
Outsourcing work?	___	___
Purchasing tools to enhance performance?	___	___
Increasing training?	___	___
Adjusting performance standards?	___	___
Working with key stakeholders?	___	___
Focusing on key milestone dates?	___	___
33. Do you consider the following options for improving monitoring and controlling:		
Determining necessary project controls?	___	___
Establishing gate reviews?	___	___
Determining meetings and setting up standardized agendas?	___	___
Determining data and information to track past cost and schedule performance?	___	___
Determining data and information to monitor cost and schedule performance?	___	___
Obtaining the best tool to collect and compile progress data?	___	___
Determining key considerations for status collection, for example, reporting period, time units, rates?	___	___
Establishing processes and procedures for collecting status?	___	___
Determining key variances requiring attention?	___	___
Tailoring reports to the needs of stakeholders?	___	___
Establishing earned value management?	___	___
Determining key actions to perform recovery planning, for example, corrective action, replanning?	___	___
34. If you are thinking about applying some aspects of Agile, did you consider		
Applying incremental development?	___	___
Breaking up each release into iterations?	___	___
Conducting daily stand-ups?	___	___
Be willing to adapt to changing requirements?	___	___
Building a prototype, or model?	___	___
Using burn down charts?	___	___
Focusing on product backlog?	___	___
Communicating face to face?	___	___
Applying the rolling wave concept?	___	___
Yielding some decision-making autonomy to the team?	___	___
Facilitating, not dominating?	___	___
Co-locating teams?	___	___
Using iteration review meetings?	___	___
Assigning dedicated team members?	___	___
35. Did you determine whether you are facing issues related to Globalization?	___	___

Question	Yes	No
Virtual teams?	——	——
Outsourcing?	——	——
Compliance?	——	——
36. Is there a danger that any of the following potential causes of idea squashing exist:		
Groupthink?	——	——
Ostracism?	——	——
Mind guards?	——	——
Organizational culture?	——	——
Economic conditions?	——	——
Mental filtering?	——	——
Not listening?	——	——
Positive incentives?	——	——
Negative incentives?	——	——
Apathy?	——	——
Your behavior?	——	——
Ego?	——	——
Tendency to action?	——	——
37. When generating ideas, do you use		
de Bono's Hat Thinking?	——	——
Brainstorming?	——	——
Mind mapping?	——	——
Critical thinking?	——	——

5

Evaluate

5.1 AN OVERVIEW

Evaluate, shown in Figure 5.1, is the fourth key action. Its entire purpose is to look at all available options to turn around a project in trouble and then select the best ones to implement.

Evaluate involves three conceptually simple activities that are, in reality, difficult to execute, shown in Figure 5.2.

4.1 *Conduct a thorough risk assessment.* At this point, the options have been determined and are under consideration for implementation. Before selection, you may recall that you along with your team considered the risks associated with each option. However, that was done at a high level. This risk assessment is an attempt to identify and evaluate risks in greater detail to ensure more effective planning for the next key action, 5.0 Execute.

4.2 *Select one or more options.* Under certain circumstances, you and your team may select multiple options to deal with a multitude of problems, issues, and challenges. This activity is where energy, vision, and choices converge to determine the best approach for recovery.

4.3 *Present and negotiate proposals.* Armed with facts and data, you are ready to present your findings and recommendations to key stakeholders. You will need to do that to generate support for proceeding to the next action, 5.0 Execute. Due to the differing interests of the stakeholders, you can expect to negotiate with some of them, especially in regard to resources and priorities. Once you receive their buy-in, you can proceed to develop a realistic plan for recovery.

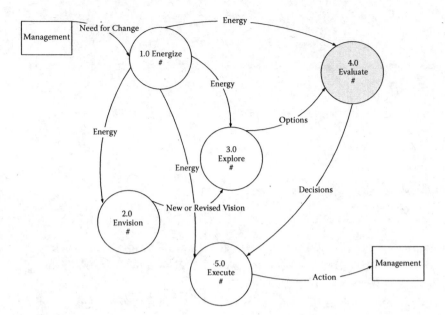

FIGURE 5.1
Level One Overview: Evaluate.

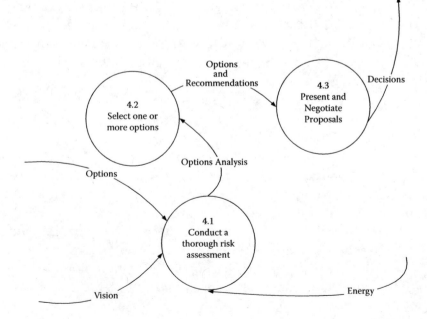

FIGURE 5.2
Level Two: Evaluate.

5.2 4.1: CONDUCT A THOROUGH RISK ASSESSMENT

You and your core team should conduct an in-depth risk assessment of each option that was selected. The primary purpose of this assessment is to determine the threats associated with each option and factor in those risks into the overall score for each option.

The risk assessment should cover a wide range of risks, including those associated with cost, schedule, and quality. You should ascertain whether risks impact four areas: systems, tools, data, and people.

A primary benefit of performing a risk assessment for each option is determining the opportunities and threats associated with each option and, in turn, factoring them in when making the final selection. It also allows you to maximize any potential gain and generate risk plans to deal with threats.

There is a secondary benefit. You and your team members can factor in risks for the overall score underlying each option. This score will reflect an adjustment that accounts for their impact on the efficiency and effectiveness of any option. Ideally, you and your team will have performed due diligence when making a selection.

Fundamentally, you can take one or both approaches toward risk management: qualitative or quantitative.

Qualitative risk management enables you to take a subjective approach when performing risk assessment, meaning essentially that mathematics is relegated to a minimal role and human judgment plays a more significant role. It requires assessing the likelihood and impact of a risk and then determining the appropriate response. You can perform a qualitative risk assessment either as an individual or with a group. Obviously, qualitative risk management works best with a group, simply because you get different viewpoints regarding the likelihood and impact of a risk.

Quantitative risk management requires taking a more objective approach toward risk assessment, though subjectivity is not altogether eliminated but minimized. You determine the probability, for example, 0 through 1, and impact of a risk, which is often those identified as significant during qualitative risk management. However, you do not necessarily have to perform qualitative risk management before performing quantitative risk management. The power of quantitative risk management is that it allows you to determine the size of the contingency (the amount of time or money set aside, for example) to deal with a risk should it occur.

Whether you have a project in trouble or a new project, you should seriously consider applying risk management. You will find it an effective tool to help you deal with problems before they arise; in other words, you and your team will be proactive, not reactive.

5.3 4.2: SELECT ONE OR MORE OPTIONS

Selecting an option requires you and your team members to remain objective and independent, if possible. Otherwise, bias can tarnish the decision. Bias, for example, in turn, can result in selecting an option that satisfies prejudices but does not effectively address the source of the problem.

The two primary objectives of this action are to achieve objectivity and independence when selecting options. Lose either one or both, and you and your team will lose credibility. As you attempt to evaluate different options, be aware of some of the subtle and overt threats to your objectivity and independence. You need to be aware of them because sooner or later someone will question the validity of your selection and, in rare cases, your motives. Failure to recognize these influences can result in selecting one or more options that can eventually put your project back in trouble after you thought you had turned it around. That's why you need to be aware of them and take action to counteract the following threats.

Management style. The tone starts at the top, so goes a common corporate truism. Management style can very well influence the selection of options. In a traditional, hierarchical environment, the tone can limit options. Any eventual selection of options could reflect management expectations, not necessarily the best options. These expectations can be overt or they can be subtle. For example, management may traditionally give specific directions on what it wants or allows or let its previous decisions set precedents on what options are permissible.

Culture. Often correlated with management style, culture—reflected in the way of doing business according to beliefs, values, norms, and mores—can influence the selection of options. A risk-averse culture, for example, will likely encourage options that represent a conservative selection, for example, an option with a high probability of success and high payback. A risk-taking culture will likely embrace options that bring the project to what some people would refer to as the razor's edge—an option, for example, that may have a low probability of success but can have a huge positive impact if it does succeed.

Personal biases. Pressure to restrict consideration of options comes not just from without but also from within. Everyone is a product of their past, time, and place. These influences can seriously impact independence and objectivity without your even realizing it. For example, project managers come from many fields, such as finance and information technology, and these experiences can influence what options are eventually selected. The reason is that many people often go with options with which they are most familiar. The result is that options are selected that may be equivalent to, as an old saying goes, putting a square peg in a round hole.

Time pressure. Projects in trouble often face tremendous pressure to turn around negative performance. Management seeks a quick turnaround because as a project continues to languish, money and time, for example, get wasted. Unfortunately, the push for a quick turnaround may have short-term positive results but also long-term negative consequences. Project managers facing tough deadlines will likely pick options under duress that could result in the long-term costs exceeding the short-term gains.

Peer pressure. The pressure to conform within a group can compromise independence and objectivity. Groupthink can create an illusion of reality, resulting in selection of an option that may not effectively turn around a project. Another frequent example of peer pressure is the danger of being labeled "not a team player." Such pressures can compromise objectivity and independence, too.

Adherence to processes and procedures. Most established organizations have standard operating processes and procedures that they follow for their daily operations and when managing projects. These processes and procedures can add great value, but they also have downsides. They can prevent people from thinking outside the box. People must follow a prescribed way of doing business, which can restrict their selection of options. For example, project managers may be restricted to looking at only certain options due to constraints imposed by procurement processes and procedures. Another example may be compliance with regulations that restrict the technological options available for consideration.

History. As mentioned earlier, all organizations are products of not only their present circumstances but also of their past. The past can restrict which options to consider. For example, a company may have historically considered using a specific type of database management system and, consequently, will not consider other options. Although this sentiment seems to have vanished now, a common statement in the information technology arena was that you could never get shot for going with IBM, an obvious statement that restricts the selection of vendors.

Your style. Your biases are not the only factor that can influence your selection of options. The way you go about dealing with people and addressing issues can influence the selection of options. For example, intense, reactive project managers will likely pursue a limited set of options; analysis is not part of their style. On the other hand, some project managers may be super-analytical, compiling an innumerable array of options but never making a decision. The key is to be aware of your current style of doing business and how it may influence your decisions.

So, what are some ways of overcoming these influences?

One method is to seek an outside opinion. You can consult with people who do not have a direct, vested interest in the outcome of your project. They can come from other projects, another organization, and even from outside of the company. They can express their insight on each option and may even come up with an option that was not considered.

Another method is to conduct research on each option. Articles in professional journals; lessons learned from similar projects in your company; case studies in books; and data research and benchmarking studies by think tanks can offer insights about each option and, again, help identify additional options.

Still another method is to take a devil's advocate approach to each option. Everything has pros and cons. For each option, identify its strengths and weaknesses using something like force field analysis, an approach for identifying the forces for and against a decision or action. No option should be exempt from scrutiny.

Being aware of the above influences enables you to begin evaluating and selecting the best option or options for recovering your project. Many of the same tools and techniques to identify options are also relevant when evaluating and selecting the best options.

We have already described the techniques that can be used to evaluate options: analogies, metaphors, and similes; synectics; nominal group technique; and Crawford slip technique. However, there are others that have not been discussed: Delphi approach, weighting options, prioritization matrix, force field analysis, and forced choice technique.

> *Delphi approach.* Developed by the Rand Corporation, a major think tank, this approach can be used to select options by developing a questionnaire and distributing it several times until a consensus is reached. The primary advantage of the Delphi approach is that it offsets peer pressure; the major disadvantage is that it is time consuming and lacks the necessary spontaneity among participants to piggyback ideas off one another.
>
> *Force field analysis.* This technique enables you and your team to evaluate options to improve performance. It is predicated on a Newtonian law of physics: for every action there is an equal reaction. For every option, there are forces that will embrace it and there are forces that will react against it. By accounting for both forces, you can select options that will likely have a more favorable chance of becoming a reality upon implementation.
>
> *Prioritization matrix.* This approach allows you to categorize options based on the relationship between two variables. The variables depend on what you and your team perceive as key determinants when selecting options. For example, efficiency and effectiveness could be two variables. Figure 5.3 shows an example of a prioritization matrix.
>
> *Weighting options table.* The weighting options table is a mathematical approach to selecting two or more options. Each option is given a weight and then assessed a value; weight and value are multiplied to derive an overall score for each item. The assigned weight is often the same for each option; the assessed value is the key determinant. Then, combined with some other technique, such as the Delphi approach, options with the same scores are further evaluated by subject matter experts to determine the best ones. Figure 5.4 shows an example of a weighted options table.
>
> *Forced choice technique.* This approach requires forcibly choosing between two or more options, ultimately ending up with a score for all the options under consideration. This technique is based on the assumption that some options are more important than others, using

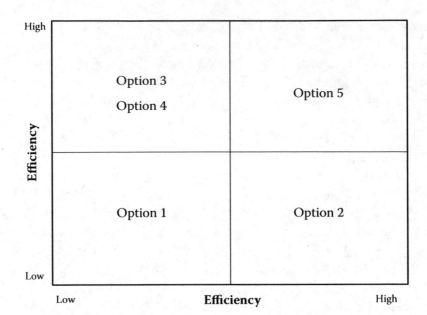

FIGURE 5.3
Prioritization matrix.

Evaluation	Weight	Assigned Value					Score
		5	4	3	2	1	
Option 1	5	5					25
Option 2	2		4				8
Option 3	3			3			9
Option 4	4				5		20
Option 5	1					2	2

FIGURE 5.4
Weighting options table.

feedback from team members. Specifically, each option is compared with the others by asking which one is more important. For example, is it Option 1 or Option 2? Team members might split points (usually a range from 0 to 5 points) between both, such as 3 points for Option 1 and 2 points for Option 2.

The negative side to this approach is that if the options are too numerous, the team can become jaded quite quickly. The upside is that it forces

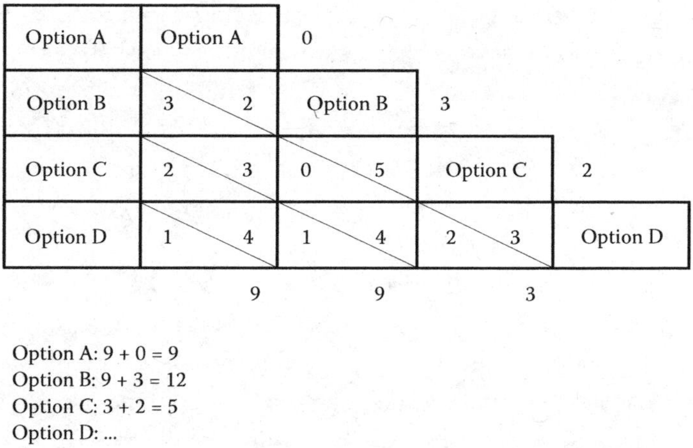

Option A	Option A	0				
Option B	3 \ 2	Option B	3			
Option C	2 \ 3	0 \ 5	Option C	2		
Option D	1 \ 4	1 \ 4	2 \ 3	Option D		
	9	9	3			

Option A: 9 + 0 = 9
Option B: 9 + 3 = 12
Option C: 3 + 2 = 5
Option D: ...

FIGURE 5.5
Forced choice technique.

people to think about the choices that they have made. Figure 5.5 is an example of a forced choice approach.

Objectivity is important to ensure that bias is minimized. Independence allows you and your team to maintain enough psychological distance from organizational pressures to avoid influencing your decisions.

One of the best ways to help minimize bias and maximize independence and objectivity is to develop and apply weighting criteria against options. The criteria should be applied uniformly and consistently.

Unfortunately, many project managers and team members do not go through the rigor of applying weighted criteria. They find that it takes too much time and effort to develop and apply. Instead, they decide on an option and move on with it. The consequences of this approach can be severe. The price of convenience, for example, can cause people to select an option that worsens problems later on in the life cycle. Trying to recover later will be more costly and difficult because the project will have acquired momentum, and the narrow focus will preclude making any changes.

To use weighted criteria, you and your team members should stick to the following guidelines.

First, define the problem or issue under consideration. This definition should be precise to ensure that the eventual selected options address a true need.

Second, consider the contextual factors in the criteria. Issues of scalability, cost, practicality, market conditions, and resistance to change are just a few factors.

Third, apply weighting criteria consistently. Avoid making exceptions in the applying criteria when taking a decision; otherwise, bias will permeate the decision. "Making an exception here and making an exception there" leads only to a bunch of exceptions, rendering the entire effort futile. Once bias takes over, objectivity and independence disappear.

A rigorous, disciplined approach in using weighted criteria offers several benefits.

First, as stressed frequently already, it minimizes the possibility of bias influencing a decision. Of course, eliminating bias is impossible because all weighting activities are by nature based on assumptions, perceived facts, and data judged more important than others. The use of weighted criteria demonstrates due diligence in trying to achieve objectivity.

Second, it provides an organized way to obtain input from several people and then compile the results of that feedback to select options. Simply asking for input without an organized approach will likely result in pushback over your selection and encourage intense disagreement later on when implementing any options. Most people will consent to a decision if they perceive if it was made in a fair, reasonable, and objective manner. Without an organized approach, the selection of an option appears muddled and random, thereby creating a lack of confidence in the decision.

Third, it allows revisiting the criteria later on to determine the rationale for selecting options. The rationale is supported with an audit trail to refine, if necessary, the decision. This audit trail is not only important to cover one's back, but it also functions as a learning tool for people making similar decisions in the future.

5.4   4.3: PRESENT AND NEGOTIATE OPTIONS

Once you've done your due diligence in generating proposals, you are ready to present one or more options for recovering your project to key stakeholders. You will need to have all your facts and data prior to your engagements with them. Your tool for doing that is preparing a Situation-Target-Proposal (STP).

An STP is a report with the expressed purpose of describing a problem, challenge, or current (As-Is) situation; a future state (To-Be), or target; and a proposal for transitioning from the current state to the future one.

The STP offers two primary benefits. It gives visibility to the work to recover your project. Another benefit is that it seeks, and hopefully obtains, management's buy-in to improve performance, thereby reducing resistance.

The situation segment of an STP describes the current state of your project. It describes in detail issues, challenges, risks, etc., with categories such as people, processes, systems, and data. These challenges may be internal or external to the project.

Be careful to distinguish between causes and symptoms for issues, challenges, and risks. For example, people challenges may be reflected in high turnover, skill shortage, or poor morale; processes with too many reviews and approvals; systems running incompatible, proprietary applications; and data being incomplete, inaccurate, or unavailable so that key decisions about the project cannot be taken. All of these, depending on your analysis, may be causes, while others may be symptoms.

Causes are the major contributors to issues, problems, and challenges and manifest themselves as symptoms. Identifying the true causes of challenges or problems is critical so that whatever options you eventually select, they actually fix them. The idea is that you want to avoid having to repeat confronting the same issues, problems, and challenges once again later in the project life cycle.

The target segment describes the To-Be, or future state, to address the issue, problem, or challenge. It is prescriptive, meaning it's where the project ought to be. You can use the same four categories of people, data, systems, and processes as a way of describing the To-Be. Of course, you can add or delete categories, depending on your needs.

Also, you should highlight the major benefits of the To-Be. These benefits should emphasize how they would fix the issues, problems, shortcomings, and challenges of the current state. Because this is an STP for a project, be sure to also discuss benefits from cost, schedule, quality, risk, and scope perspectives.

The proposal segment explains your plans to move from the current state to the future state. Here, you present the options that you and your team chose during 4.0: Evaluate action. These options should address all the challenges and problems identified in the situation segment of your report.

If you need direction from management on the options, be sure to note it in this segment. If you like a host of options from which to choose from, however, be prepared to give a recommendation in case management asks for your opinion. For each option, provide a brief description and note any issues, risks, or other challenges.

There is one option that you need to consider, no matter how unsettling it may be; that option is terminating your project. That option may be in the interests of the organization, but it will be difficult to even mention for several reasons.

Fear of job loss. Naturally, few people want to lose their jobs. If everyone is in a matrix organization, then an option to kill the project may not be as threatening as someone who is hard-lined to the project. The former will have a place to go, either back to the home organization or to another project; the latter will have to seek a new position. Either way, you can expect the morale and esprit de corps to plummet, and your popularity, to say the least, will do the same.

Ego. Not only is your ego invested in the project, but so is that of the team members. They have probably invested considerable time, effort, and emotion up to this point in the project, and any mention of killing the project is proof that their previous work did not meet expectations. Your ego, too, could be affected because it is an indirect admission that you do not have the confidence to recover the project.

Unwillingness to admit failure. Some people cannot admit failure; it goes against the grain. They will fight to the very end, and the very thought of admitting failure is anathema to their psyche. Management does not, for example, like to admit failure—nor does just about anyone else. Yet, a project can really be a dismal failure, and to invest additional time, money, and effort only prolongs the failure. Consequently, everyone involved with the project continues to suffer.

Strong belief in the outcome of the project. This is closely allied to the preceding point; certain stakeholders believe in the vision so much that they are unwilling to admit that it can't be achieved. An illusion persists that maybe with a stroke of genius or a silver bullet, the project will recover. Granted, the sheer determination of a team can turn around a project. Sometimes that does occur; more often, it doesn't.

Empire building. Cancel a project, and more than team members lose their position. Executives who supported the project may see it as a way to add to their power base. More people and money, for example, often translate into greater power for themselves and their organizations. Ideally, executives look after the interests of their organization; often, though, they manage to interleave their interests with those of the organization. One thing is certain about human nature. People who acquire position and power hate to give it up; canceling a project poses a threat.

No alternative. Canceling a project may involve returning to the status quo, which may or may not be acceptable to key stakeholders. There is no other choice; to do otherwise may invite legal and financial ramifications. Compliance projects are a prime example. If the government mandates an action, such as Sarbanes-Oxley, the project cannot be terminated without severe consequences.

Killing a project is one of the hardest decisions to make. As the project manager taking over a troubled project, you may have to consider that option. True, your coming aboard is an admission that management wants to save the project. However, management is usually not that close to the project—at least not to the degree that you are. It will take considerable courage on your part to even mention the option to terminate your project.

Each of the segments of the STP can be a diagram rather than a narrative description, or it can be a combination of both. It can also take the form of a bullet chart.

You can add two additional segments to the STP, if desired.

The first addition is Help Needed. Here, you list any issues, problems, or challenges that management needs to help you and your team to resolve. They could be a request for additional assistance that you cannot handle, or approvals to acquire capital equipment.

The other addition is Next Steps. In this segment, you let management know what you'll be doing next, which will likely be developing and executing plans based on management's approval of the STP.

Getting acceptance of the STP does not mean you are in the clear. You will still have to face the grim reality of negotiating for people, budget, tools, and other support. For instance, you may have to negotiate with the customer over availability of time commitment. Or you may have to negotiate with functional managers to release the people who happen to be supporting other projects of equivalent importance. So, keep the following negotiating point in mind because you will be doing a lot of it with stakeholders such as vendors, team members, steering committee members, or sponsor. Remember this point: Expression of support does not mean actual support.

One, seek a win-win solution. Initially, you may have the opportunity to acquire the resources you need or have the freedom to run your project. You may have an informal or formal position of power to do your job. However, be careful that you don't run over people, especially key stakeholders. It is best to seek a win-win solution in most or all of your negotiations for the simple reason that you do not want to alienate key stakeholders, or worse, make them enemies; they could sabotage your efforts when you least suspect it.

Two, pursue interests, not position. When negotiating, try to understand the interests of the other party and present your requests from that perspective. Winning negotiations is far easier if you are able to satisfy the other party's interests as well as your own.

Three, to realize the previous point, try to learn about the other party's background, needs, and interests in as much detail as possible. The more you know about the other party, the greater will be your ability to achieve a win-win result. If you get too much information, determine what aspects of it are useful and what can be disregarded. Your objectives in the negotiation will help you make that determination. You will hopefully have enough information to make that a reality.

Four, have a strategy in mind when negotiating; that is, know what your goals and objectives are and how you plan to achieve them. Knowing what you want, ironically, tells you what you can give up. As a side note, try to ascertain the other party's strategy, too; you will be able to address objections as well as obtain an agreement that is a win-win result for you and the other party.

Five, have a backup plan. Be a good risk manager in this regard. If you cannot make an impression on the other party, you will need to determine some alternative courses of action. A backup plan allows you to negotiate on equal terms with the other party, and sometimes even from a position of strength. It also enables you to at least avoid the feeling that all is lost if you fail to negotiate successfully.

Finally, and related to the previous point, you must be willing to walk away. Sometimes, it is better to reach no agreement than to get into one that can hurt the recovery of your project. An example is negotiating a bad contractual relationship with a vendor that might, for example, cost or delay the recovery effort later on. Having a backup plan will give you the strength to walk away.

5.5 CONCLUSION

It is important to reiterate that you and your team members need to strive to maintain objectivity and independence when making evaluations and selections. Failure to do so will tarnish the credibility of your decisions and your reputation, thereby making meaningful, substantive change difficult. Of course, time frequently neither allows for this degree of analytical rigor, nor will such an effort guarantee sufficient payback. However, short of an emergency, most situations should allow for time to perform some objective, independent analysis. If lack of time or cost is frequently an issue, then it might indicate a more salient, deep-rooted problem that, ironically, requires a more thorough analysis to determine the best options to deploy.

Case Study (*Continued*)

Evaluate. In the afternoon of the second day, the team was ready to start the evaluation of each of the options. Deborah emphasized the need for the team to remain as objective as possible to ward off any biases. She also had the team determine the best way to approach the options, and the consensus was to use the nominal group technique. Once the team applied the SWOT (Strengths, Weaknesses, Options, Threats) approach to each option, they voted on ranking the options from the most to the least important. Deborah then compiled the selection and presented the results to reflect the ranking of the options. She then compared it to the revised vision of the project to ensure that the results addressed its major goals and objectives.

Deborah then asked the team to help her draft the content of a Situation-Target-Proposal. Using a brainstorming session along with the information already generated by the team, the scribe recorded notes as she asked questions (along with the others) until the team felt satisfied with the content. She then said she would schedule another meeting with the team to develop a plan based on the feedback from the steering team.

Deborah met with the steering team, which included key management personnel from her organization and the customer's organization as well as the project sponsor. The steering team, for the most part, accepted the STP and was impressed with the results. However, the STP was still not convincing because it did not contain a business case for the project based on the new parameters. A downturn in the economy was occurring, it emphasized, and if the project could not demonstrate a substantial financial benefit in a relatively short period of time, it would have to be terminated.

The consequences, of course, of termination would be substantial; people would lose their jobs but, just as importantly, an extremely important application would not be built, thus hurting the reputation of the company. She knew that the business case, based on sound financial analysis, would be the driving force for continuing the project. Immediately, she reconvened the core team and explained the results of the steering committee. The team agreed, therefore, that it would operate on some basic assumptions and use them to develop a high project plan, including time and cost estimates; a work breakdown structure at the tier 3 level, assignments with existing team members, and a network diagram. She explored with the team the use of fast tracking and crashing as a way to move back the project completion date. The content of the plans would be used to generate a business case for the project. Deborah procured the services of a business analyst from the company's finance organization to develop the business case, addressing return on investment (ROI), internal rate of return (IRR), and the payback period.

Once the business case was complete, Deborah reviewed it with the core team for any additional input. Some revisions were made, and it was packaged with the STP and presented to the steering committee. The steering committee approved, despite the fact that one of the options included terminating the project.

5.6 GETTING-STARTED CHECKLIST

Question	Yes	No
1. Will you conduct a thorough risk assessment of each option?	____	____
2. Which approach to risk assessment will you take:		
Qualitative approach?	____	____
Quantitative approach?	____	____
3. Are you aware of some of the major influences that can affect your selection of options, such as		
Management style?	____	____
Culture?	____	____
Personal biases?	____	____
Time pressure?	____	____
Peer pressure?	____	____

Question	Yes	No
Adherence to processes and procedures?	___	___
History?	___	___
Your style?	___	___
4. Are you considering ways to overcome influences, such as		
Seeking an outside opinion?	___	___
Conducting research about each option?	___	___
Taking a devil's advocate approach?	___	___
5. Are you considering the use of one or more of the following techniques for selecting options, such as		
Analogies?	___	___
Metaphors?	___	___
Similes?	___	___
Synectics?	___	___
Nominal group technique?	___	___
Weighting options?	___	___
Crawford slip technique?	___	___
Delphi approach?	___	___
Force field analysis?	___	___
Prioritization matrix?	___	___
Forced choice technique?	___	___
6. When putting together a Situation-Target-Proposal (STP), will you		
Describe the To-Be, or end state, for the problem or challenge being addressed?	___	___
Highlight the major benefits of the To-Be?	___	___
Describe the As-Is and its shortcomings?	___	___
Describe the options?	___	___
Include, if necessary, direction from management on options?	___	___
Identify help needed?	___	___
Describe next steps?	___	___
7. When negotiating for resources to implement options that you select, do you		
Seek a win-win solution?	___	___
Pursue mutual interests, not position?	___	___
Learn about the other party's background?	___	___
Have a strategy in mind when negotiating?	___	___
Have a backup plan?	___	___
Prepare yourself mentally to walk away?	___	___
8. Will you account for some of the reasons why the option to terminate the project may not be selected, such as		
Fear of job loss?	___	___
Ego?	___	___
Unwillingness to admit failure?	___	___

Question	Yes	No
Strong belief in the outcome of the project?	____	____
Empire building?	____	____
No alternative?	____	____

6

Execute

6.1 AN OVERVIEW

At this point, you, your team, and other key stakeholders should support the vision described in your Situation-Target-Proposal (S-T-P). It is now time to turn the new or revised vision into reality by performing the next action, Execute, shown in Figure 6.1.

The key is to implement solid project management concepts, tools, techniques, and methods to *execute* the project. In all likelihood, many of them were ineffectively implemented or missing in the first place, contributing to the current deplorable state of affairs.

Execute requires performing five fundamental activities as shown in Figure 6.2. These are

5.1: Develop a realistic recovery plan.
5.2: Apply knowledge of what people can and cannot do.
5.3: Get participation and commitment from stakeholders.
5.4: Apply project execution practices.

Using the options selected in the previous action, you and your team can perform 5.1: Develop a realistic recovery plan. This activity involves replacing or fixing the previous schedule (if a previous one even existed). Then, you are ready to make new or revised assignments by performing 5.2: Apply knowledge of what people can or cannot do. This activity should be relatively straightforward because of information collected during the previous actions. It is at this point that the people performing the assignments can provide additional feedback on their tasks, and you can make the corresponding adjustments.

Once the team provides feedback and reconciles differences, you and your team can perform 5.3: Get participation and commitment from stakeholders.

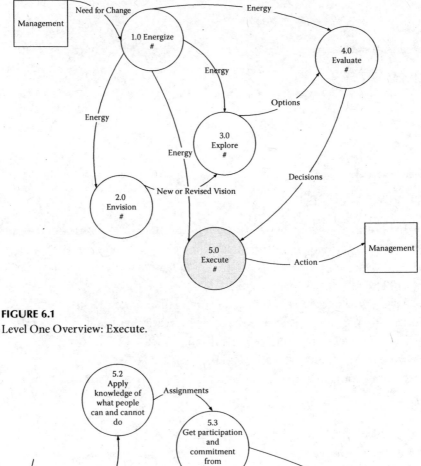

FIGURE 6.1
Level One Overview: Execute.

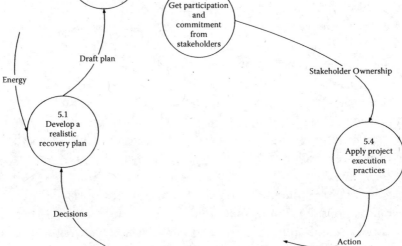

FIGURE 6.2
Level Two: Execute.

This activity requires ensuring that all roles, responsibilities, and authorities are complete and that the plan has been adequately defined.

Finally, you and your entire team execute the plan by performing activity 5.4: Apply project execution practices. This activity follows the plan and tracks performance and, when necessary, takes corrective action.

6.2 5.1: DEVELOP A REALISTIC RECOVERY PLAN

At this point, the new or revised vision and processes, tools, techniques, etc., have been incorporated into a plan. It is also at this point that risks are accounted for and measures are instituted to ensure that if a major risk arises, the team will be able to deal with it. When implementing the new plan, of course, it is important that you and your team maintain dialogue with key stakeholders; failure to do so will only lead subsequently to pushback by key stakeholders who were not consulted.

A new plan offers two benefits:

1. It builds confidence among all the key participants and especially among team members and the customer. The combination of a vision in the form of a charter and a plan will tell members not only what they will achieve but also how they will approach it. Because they have provided feedback and now have ownership, they will be less reluctant to oppose the vision or plan. There may be differences, naturally, but the divisions will likely be less in magnitude and number as the new vision and plan go into effect.
2. There will also likely be a new management style on the project. The original management style probably had a significant negative impact. Using a more collaborative, communicative approach to generating a new charter and plan is likely a different approach from the one employed earlier. This time, the feedback from the key stakeholders is reflected in the vision and plan, resulting in "our" plan rather than "your" plan.

A key decision at this point is to determine the breadth and depth of the project management disciplines, tools, and techniques to apply on your project as described in your new project management plan. Their decision should not be taken lightly.

If project management is applied too lightly, then the project could experience the same problems it faced earlier, resulting once again in a project in trouble. If applied with too heavy a hand, then an "administrative" burden could be levied on the project, slowing it down and resulting in the project slipping into trouble once again, but for the opposite reason. Either way, the wrong approach could add risks to a project and endanger progress.

Unfortunately, no algorithm exists that you can apply. No hard-and-fast rules exist that will give you a yes-or-no answer. Only judgments made by you, your team, and your management can provide guidance. This judgment should be based on a number of factors, however.

Size. Size can vary according to cost, geography, complexity, and scope. The "bigger" the project, the more rigorous the project management disciplines to implement in terms of breadth and depth. Large projects involving, for example, hundreds of people and millions of dollars of costs over a five-year period, will require more project management than one that costs $50,000 people, involves five people, and must be completed in two months.

Execution time. The time available to deliver a product or service will determine the breadth and depth of project management to apply. If you have a two-month delivery, your rudimentary project management practices will likely suffice. If it's a two-year delivery, more project management may be necessary.

Team size. Adding more people adds more complexity and diversity, thus requiring more project management disciplines. As more people join a project, the number of channels for coordination and communication increases. The greater the depth and breadth of project management, the greater the oversight needed to keep people focused on the vision, goals, and objectives. For a small team, the breadth and depth of project management required will be less.

Importance. The more important your project is to the organization, the more project management disciplines will be necessary. Management will need evidence that you are exercising sufficient discipline and will want formal reporting. Management and its leadership need to be assured by the application of project management disciplines that the project will deliver on time, within budget, and with the highest quality. For projects of lower importance and less visibility, the degree of rigor in applying project management disciplines will be much less.

Degree of schedule flexibility. A project with significant milestones that cannot be missed will require more project management discipline than a project with flexible milestones. In the former case, management may be nervous about the consequences of late delivery, for example, penalty payments, decline in stock value, that it will want to feel confident that sufficient project management rigor will be applied on the project. Less schedule flexibility requires greater attention to detail to ensure that the schedule is met and that when slides do occur, you can anticipate the degree of the impact and respond, not react, appropriately.

Risk. A project whose failure will have potentially a big impact on an organization requires applying more breadth and depth of project management disciplines than one whose failure will have a smaller impact. For high-risk projects, more project management demonstrates due diligence, meaning that the organization is doing what is reasonable and necessary, for example, planning, to ensure success in the future; due care is the actual application of disciplines to demonstrate commitment. For high-risk projects, failure can cause the stock price to decline significantly, for example. Due diligence and due care serve as insurance policies to provide stockholders and executive management with the confidence that you are in control.

When determining the scalability of project management, remember that both too much and too little project management disciplines will have positive and negative consequences, from the perspective of cost, schedule, and quality. For that reason, you should work closely with key stakeholders, such as your customer, core team, and executive sponsor to determine the appropriate breadth and depth of the project management disciplines to be applied. This generates a greater sense of ownership and commitment to those disciplines rather than you having to sell their value repeatedly.

The trend is toward a lighter implementation of traditional project management practices for small and even medium-sized projects. This trend is adopted from Agile methodologies, and the project management aspects are referred to as PM Light. Agile, though associated with information systems development, may actually be what your project needs—in part or in its entirety.

In all fairness, and with some merit, project management is sometimes viewed as bureaucratic. To a large degree, this is a misperception; it is often the result of viewing project management as "one-size-fits-all" or, as Henry Ford once said, "You can have any color you want as long as it's black."

Agile methods can help to overcome that misperception, as long as it is applied to complement project management. Here are some useful guidelines, concepts, tools, and techniques from Agile methodology that you might want to consider applying in various ways to execute the recovery of your project:

Apply incremental development. You might decide to reduce the size of the product or service, building upon it over several releases during a specific time span. This approach enables the team to deliver a product or service within their capabilities and reduces the chance of underdelivery.

Break each release into iterations. This is tied closely to the previous point; each iteration has a set of tasks and corresponding deliverables that are produced in short time periods, such as every two weeks or monthly. If the content of an iteration can't be met, it slides into the next iteration for a given release.

Conduct daily standups. Although rarely popular, this technique encourages people to talk about what they did the previous day, what they will be doing the rest of the day, and raise issues, problems, or challenges that they have experienced from the previous day. The purpose of the standup is, however, to share information and not solve problems.

Be willing to adapt to changing requirements. You and your team should expect change to happen, especially in an environment that is highly dynamic. Change is the centerpiece of Agile because the emphasis is on meeting the needs of the customer, who is often undecided and fickle. Of course, adapting to change does not mean randomly accepting it. It does mean applying effective change control to determine the cost, schedule, and scope impacts of the change. The team works closely with the customer to determine the impacts of the change, and the latter decides whether it is feasible.

Build a prototype, or model. You use the prototype first to gather requirements and then make key decisions on how to proceed. The building of a prototype enables both the team and the customer to see results quickly and make the necessary changes to satisfy requirements. The idea here is to avoid long time periods before something is delivered to the customer. Using a prototype approach provides feedback more quickly because it delivers tangible results faster.

Use burn-down charts. A burn-down chart is a physical count of items produced over a time period. These items, often tangible although not required, show how much of something has been produced and how much remains in the time remaining. Burn-downs can also be used as a complement to schedules and, under Agile, are often viewed as being more useful than a schedule. The emphasis is on completing physical units and not flow time.

Focus on product backlog. There is a good chance that your project has a backlog of work to complete, reflected in a sliding schedule. Under Agile, the project manager works with the customer to determine the priority of the remaining work to complete. The idea is that the customer decides priority and the content, not the team building the product. It also forces the customer to distinguish between what it needs versus what it wants.

Communicate face to face. A major emphasis in Agile is ongoing communication with the customer. There is less emphasis on producing voluminous documentation before proceeding. Instead, the customer works constantly with the team to develop the final deliverables through constant communication regarding direction and feedback. There is less emphasis on documentation as a means of communication and more emphasis on face-to-face interaction.

Apply the rolling wave concept. There is no need to have to plan everything completely before starting the work. You and your team can apply the rolling wave concept, that is, plan the current phase or release, but only plan the remaining work when you know more. This approach enables starting the work earlier and more quickly as well as providing an opportunity to refine the plan as the project progresses.

Yield some decision-making autonomy to the team. A tendency exists for project managers to think that they make all the decisions, big and small. This attitude can kill progress, especially if a backlog of decisions grows, either because project managers are indecisive or they "upload" the decisions up the hierarchy. It is also harmful for the team's morale, as team members yearn to proceed.

Under Agile, the team is granted more autonomy to make decisions, particularly technical ones, without having to wait for the project manager. By delegating more decision making to team members, they gain a greater sense of ownership and commitment while you concentrate on other important matters or decisions.

Facilitate, not dominate. This is tied to the previous point; you become more of a facilitator than a dominator on your project. You focus on doing whatever is necessary, such as removing administrative roadblocks, to enable the team to accomplish its vision, goals, and objectives. Hence, the team concentrates on getting the "real work" done. You become, therefore, an instrument of the team rather than the other way around.

Co-locate teams. Although it allows the use of modern information technology, the real emphasis of Agile is on face-to-face communications and teamwork. The best way to achieve that is through co-location, meaning that everyone, including the customer, works in the same location. This not only improves communication but also increases morale and esprit de corps. The presumption is that physical proximity allows stakeholders to gel and jam, thereby reducing the time to deliver a product or service to the customer.

Use iteration review meetings. At the end of each iteration or sprint, the team conducts what is roughly equivalent to a lessons learned session. Team members not only discuss what went well but also what didn't go well, so that subsequent iterations or sprints can proceed much more smoothly. This session is also meant to share information and serve as a learning experience.

Assign dedicated team members. You may find your team members working in a matrix environment, meaning that they support more than one project. Under Agile, that is not the case; team members focus on one project—yours—for the entire life cycle. The concept is that people cannot be efficient or effective working on two more projects because they have to shift their attention and get back up to speed. It also wears down team members, who find themselves working on multiple high priorities, which is impossible because a person can focus on only one priority at a time.

Whether you use Agile or some other approach, you will have to develop a schedule. The schedule will need to have certain characteristics if it is to prove useful. Otherwise, the project may be traveling down the road leading to failure once again. Even though scheduling is an art in many respects, it is also a science that requires exhibiting certain characteristics.

One, all tasks in the schedule connect with other tasks, either as a predecessor or successor, or both. This connection enables you see the downstream impact of a slide of a task, especially ones on the critical path (those tasks that cannot slide without impacting the final completion date for the project).

Two, all tasks have a start and stop date. Both dates are based on the dependencies (e.g., predecessor, successor) among tasks, relationship types (e.g., start-to-start, finish-to-start) among them, and flow time, or duration, of each task.

Three—and this is related to the last point—no task should have a TBD (To Be Determined). A TBD, either for the start or finish dates of a task, is a prescription for failure, especially if left unaddressed for a long time. It will pose a problem sooner or later because the TBD is simply a sign of an unresolved issue; as the project proceeds through its life cycle, a TBD can soon become a critical issue, even a showstopper. TBDs are frequently a way to avoid commitment by a responsible party and start a project without delay. The only problem is that a TBD will likely later result in a delay, and at the wrong time. The only time that a TBD is permissible is when key stakeholders approve of it or when applying a specific approach that allows for it, for example, following an Agile methodology.

Four, all dates are based on the work to be done. Many projects find themselves in trouble the minute they start because the milestones are unrealistic. Failure to base a schedule on the work to be done is like putting ten pounds of groceries in a five-pound bag; sooner or later, the bag will break. Frequently, milestones are set by management, in the expectation that the project manager and the team will "make it happen." Soon, one milestone after another begins to slide, and despite the heroic efforts of the project manager and the team, the project fails. If the dates are achieved, one of the other variables of project management (e.g., cost, quality, scope) is impacted negatively.

Five, all tasks have someone assigned to perform the work. No task is left unassigned; otherwise, the task will slide until the very end; then it will turn critical, and no one will be available to perform it. If more than one person is assigned to a task, one person should be held responsible for its completion.

Six, not all tasks in a schedule are equal; some are more equal than others, and they are on the critical path. The critical path is the longest path in the schedule and contains tasks that cannot slide without impacting the overall completion date for the project. More than one critical path can exist, and you should focus on the tasks to be completed. Recognize, too, that the critical path can change as you and your team provide status reports on schedule performance.

Seven, all the tasks in the schedule should appear in the work breakdown structure, or WBS, which is a top-down listing of the work to be completed. The WBS is the authoritative document for the scope of your project and the activities to complete it. No tasks in your schedule should be different from the work packages in the WBS; otherwise, it reflects scope creep (an unintentional expansion of your project's scope).

6.3 5.2: APPLY KNOWLEDGE OF WHAT PEOPLE CAN AND CANNOT DO

The recovery plan, of course, cannot be implemented without the input of key stakeholders in general and team members in particular.

One of the most useful tools on a project is the development of a skills matrix. This tool provides excellent information about the knowledge and expertise of the individuals on the project. The information can be utilized to eventually assign people to tasks described in the work breakdown structure at the work package level.

There are essentially three steps to building a skills matrix and eventually assigning people with the requisite skills to the appropriate tasks.

> First, build a matrix that reflects the skills across the top row and then the names of team members down the far left vertical column. Then indicate in each cell the degree of strength, such as E for Expert, A for Advanced, B for Beginner, and N for None. Figure 6.3 is an example of a skills matrix.

> Second, using the skills in the previous matrix, build one that shows the skills across the top row and down the far left vertical column the work package level tasks in the work breakdown structure. Then

	Spanish	English	Persian	Mandarin
Bob	A	E	N	A
Mary	N	E	N	A
Sue	N	A	N	N
Ted	B	E	A	E
Fred	N	E	B	N

Legend
E = Expert
A = Advanced
B = Beginner
N = None

FIGURE 6.3
Skills matrix (individual degree of strength).

	Spanish	English	Persian	Mandarin
Prepare instructor guide in Spanish	A	N	N	N
Prepare instructor guide in English	N	A	N	N
Prepare instructor guide in Persian	N	N	E	N
Prepare instructor guide in Mandarin	N	N	N	E
Legend E = Expert A = Advanced B = Beginner N = None				

FIGURE 6.4
Skills matrix (needed level of expertise).

indicate in each cell the degree of relevance of that skill to each task, such as E for requires an Expert; A for Advanced; B for Beginner; and N for None. Figure 6.4 is an example of such a matrix.

Third, using the people from the first matrix and the tasks in the second matrix, create a third matrix. In this matrix, the top row will have the names of the people and the far left vertical column will have the tasks; you can then assign people to the relevant tasks. Ideally, a person with a skill at a specific level of mastery will meet the skill requirements of a specific task. For example, Joe Magnifico has A for Advanced expertise in modeling techniques. Task 74 has a requirement for a modeling expertise of A for Advanced expertise. Therefore, Joe is assigned to that task because there is a match. If Joe has a level B for Beginner and not an A for Task 74, then there is a skill deficiency; someone who can help Joe will have to be found, or that task will have to be reassigned to someone else. Figure 6.5 is an example of this matrix.

Knowing your skill needs and the expertise of your team gives you a powerful tool for utilizing the most important resource of team—your people. They have the background, knowledge, and skills that you require; if they don't, then you will know what you are missing and you can look to satisfy that shortfall.

	Bob	Mary	Sue	Ted	Fred
Prepare instructor guide in Spanish	P				
Prepare instructor guide in English		B	P		
Prepare instructor guide in Persian				B	
Prepare instructor guide in Mandarin				P	P
Legend P = Primary B = Backup					

FIGURE 6.5
Skills matrix (matching individual expertise with the needed expertise).

	Bob	Mary	Sue	Ted	Fred
Prepare instructor guide in Spanish	R				
Prepare instructor guide in English		S	R		
Prepare instructor guide in Persian				S	
Prepare instructor guide in Mandarin				R	R
Legend R = Responsible S = Support					

FIGURE 6.6
Responsibility assignment matrix.

When making assignments, you will need to use your skills matrix as a guide. The information in the matrix can help you construct another matrix called the Responsibility Assignment Matrix (RAM). The RAM tells who is assigned to which task and their level of responsibility, for example, lead, performer, etc. (see Figure 6.6).

The combination of the skills matrix and the RAM will help you address issues such as resource requirements, for example, quantities and qualities, fulfilled and lacking, lead times to procure necessary resources with the requisite characteristics, and sources for procuring missing resources.

It is important to identify, to the extent necessary, the resource requirements so that you have the resources available when you need them and in the appropriate quantity. Otherwise, key tasks in the schedule will slide, especially the ones on the critical path.

6.4 5.3: GET PARTICIPATION AND COMMITMENT FROM STAKEHOLDERS

Avoid executing a plan without the understanding of, and buy-in from, your key stakeholders. If you do, you can expect resistance if the plan interferes with plans for other projects and operations. That is probably why your project ended up in trouble in the first place.

You can gain commitment by having one-on-one schedule reviews with each stakeholder and having group sessions to resolve integration points among them. Each key stakeholder will be responsible for a set of deliverables and corresponding activities to build them. In some cases, they will have to work with other stakeholders, send deliverables to another stakeholder, or receive deliverables from yet another. Regardless, they will need to communicate and coordinate with each other, and that facilitates commitment to the schedule.

6.5 5.4: APPLY GOOD PROJECT EXECUTION PRACTICES

In theory, a system has a tendency to reach equilibrium; however, sooner or later it will deteriorate, leading to dysfunctional behavior unless actions are taken to maintain the system and even enhance its performance.

A project is a system that requires continuous maintenance to ensure that degradation does not occur. Too many times, unfortunately, disciplines are applied on projects but soon become outdated or are not followed; one of the main reasons is that people forget that the new system, in this case the project, requires constant attention and feedback on its progress to achieve the vision and execute the plan. The key is to ensure that this scenario does not occur, by exercising disciplined status collection and assessment on cost, schedule, and quality performance.

How is this achieved for status collection and assessment? Persistency and consistency.

Persistency is ensuring that status collection and assessment occur regularly. There will be a tendency to skip persistency for many reasons. Sometimes, people want to avoid the challenges and hassles of collecting and assessing status; at other times, people want to avoid facing the reality that the project may not be progressing as expected, or that some key members pride themselves on fighting fires rather than working proactively.

Consistency is applying the same approach to status collection and assessment throughout a project. It involves regularly collecting the same data, for example, and generating the same reports. This regularity occurs with data and time. The same data (if reliable and valid) is collected, and the same reports are generated during each time period. Through consistency, past and projected future performance can be evaluated for trends. Too often, project managers and other stakeholders make exceptions, thereby not only leading to erroneous, inconsistent data but also resulting in poor decisions, complexity, and firefighting.

There are many reasons for this tendency to throw out consistency. Sometimes, it may be due to prejudices entering the mindsets of certain stakeholders; and it may also be the consequence of people not seeing value in collecting and assessing status in the first place. Whatever the reason, inconsistency can result in flawed performance reporting and the project quickly sliding into reactive mode.

Applying disciplined status collection and assessment offers several benefits.

One, it provides reliable cost, schedule, and quality performance reports. When their data are reliable and valid, these reports can help effectively determine how well a project has performed, its current state, and anticipate performance in the future (assuming current progress is maintained).

Two, it allows you to proactively rather than reactively approach different situations, especially negative ones. Metrics, such as earned value reports, can help you and your team anticipate problems. The challenge, in the contemporary environment, is not a dearth of information but too much information. It is critical to establish only metrics that indicate performance on key tasks.

Three, it creates and maintains a sense of immediacy on the part of team members and other stakeholders. Through persistent and consistent status collection and assessment, people tend to pay more attention to performance, especially after providing input to help formulate plans and being held accountable for results. To ensure attention, you can provide visibility of performance metrics so that people know if their performance remains focused on the vision.

There's an old acronym that has been bandied about in the information technology (IT) world: GIGO, for Garbage In, Garbage Out. The basic premise behind it is that if the data is bad, then so will be the resulting information. Good data equals good information; bad data equals bad information.

Obtaining good data to generate good information is not easy. So many threats exist to the validity and reliability of data.

Time is one threat. With time, data can become old, no longer relevant as a tool to generate information. That is why it is critical to collect data at regular periods of time as a means of determining trends in the information. An example from a project perspective is collecting the schedule status monthly for a two-month project; the length of time is too long to give any meaningful progress on such a short-lived project.

Measurement is a threat. Without our realizing it, the very act of measuring data can influence data output. The act itself can affect what the data tells you. For example, measurement can become very selective, meaning that data used to generate information can be cherry-picked. Another example is senior management asking for status on particular tasks; as you assess the status, people come to know that those tasks are being monitored, and naturally inflate their progress.

Selection is a threat, too, one that is ever-present in sampling. The criteria you use to select data can skew the results. If you need to pull data from a database, you need to do so randomly. An example might be management wanting you to generate information on schedule performance; you pull data and generate information only within a given time frame, knowingly or unwittingly, not realizing that the selected date range generates a misperception, good or bad.

Maturation is a threat. Most project environments are in a continuous flux. The data in one period may no longer be relevant in another one. You need to account for those changes. An example: The scope of the project changes but the plans do not, causing people to misconstrue that the reports are reflective of what is actually occurring.

You will likely not be able to eliminate the threats to valid data. However, you need to recognize that threats do exist and, above all, be up front about them when reporting on performance. Otherwise, your credibility could be hurt.

With valid data, you can develop metrics that add value to you and your stakeholders.

With today's access to computing power and the tendency to save everything online, there will be the temptation to use it all and produce countless reports, including reports involving metrics. The problem is that more metrics only cause more confusion and information overload. You need to generate metrics that people can use to improve their own performance for the entire project.

What are some qualities of an effective metric?

One, it adds value for the customer and other key stakeholders. If no one uses it or understands the metric, then it will be a waste of time and effort generating it, in addition to causing confusion.

Two, it uses timely, "clean" data. A metric using flawed data will result in a lack of confidence in the result calculated. The principle of GIGO applies to metrics. As soon as the stakeholders lose faith in a metric due to bad data, then they will no longer trust any of the output. All confidence in the metric, and perhaps even in you, will be lost.

Finally, the metric should be simple. Extreme complexity is often a cover for confusion; contrary to popular belief, a complex weaving of variables and their relationships into a formula may reflect muddled thinking rather than mathematical expertise. You should strive for simplicity in your metrics. Exceptions exist; however, simplicity should be the norm.

Perhaps your most effective project management set of metrics is earned value management (EVM), an excellent tool to impart discipline and focus to a runaway project. EVM just doesn't happen by itself; it also requires discipline and focus to implement.

First, EVM requires reliable, valid data collection. Practices include finding data that is "clean," meaning that it is free of defects, for example, inaccuracies, bias; is valid, measuring what it is supposed to measure; and meets an expected standard, for example, it is timely.

Second, EVM requires collecting data consistently. This requirement means obtaining data that satisfies some qualitative criteria, for example, format, so that the resulting calculations produce dependable results. By collecting data, for instance, from disparate sources, the eventual results could mask some serious inconsistencies, producing invalid calculated results. Key stakeholders, including you and your team, could end up making important decisions based on flawed data, causing errors in judgment.

Three, data must be collected regularly, such as weekly, biweekly, and monthly. Irregular collection often results in inconsistency in reporting, which, in turn, can make it difficult to discern trends.

Four, EVM requires good tools to generate information. These tools can be spreadsheets or project management software. The larger your project, the more you'll need automated tools to generate metrics and to collect data.

Five, EVM is worthless if no one knows how to interpret the information. People will require training that not only stresses the value of EVM but also how to interpret the reports. Nothing is more damaging to the credibility of output than handing stakeholders a deck of reports that are difficult to understand and only tend to obscure rather than clarify.

Six—and this is tied to the last point—make EVM expertise available in case people have trouble using EVM or understanding the reports. Frustration up front results in frustration downstream.

EVM is especially useful for imparting discipline and focus to a runaway project. It should be realized, however, that a project is an enabler for the people on the project and not an end in itself. EVM reports, similar to all other reports, must have value to whoever receives them.

In addition to effective metrics, you will likely need to exercise three other effective disciplines while executing your recovery plan:

1. Applying change management
2. Establishing and maintaining risk management
3. Building and deploying a communications plan

Applying change management. Change is a fact of life, and more so for projects. You are going to have to implement change to bring the project around and, as you might have guessed, that is not easy.

Change, literally and figuratively, should not have to come from the barrel of a gun, as Mao Tse-Tung noted. Instead, it should come through much gentler means, which last longer. So what can you do to bring about change?

First, obtain engagement. After identifying the key stakeholders, seek to obtain their involvement in identifying and selecting options to turn around your project. Through involvement comes a reduction in resistance and an increase in commitment. After all, why would they criticize the changes if they had a hand in recommending them?

Second, implement change management procedures. These procedures can be formal or informal, but regardless, they should follow a logical approach. Once again, you should identify key stakeholders, only this time when formulating the procedures. Involvement will promote commitment to following the procedures.

Third, recognize that not all changes are equal. Changes will vary according to priority and impact. You and your team should define what constitutes a high, medium, or low change request. If all changes are treated equally, your project will fall further into trouble as you and your team move into reactive mode.

Fourth, adhere to the procedures. The sooner you make exceptions, the greater the likelihood of scope creep, that is, the gradual and unintended expansion of the scope. Change management requires discipline on everyone's part, including the customers. Lose that discipline, and it's almost certain that your project will be in trouble once again.

Finally, develop metrics. These metrics will be in addition to the typical costs and schedule metrics generated on many projects. They should cover topics such as number of priorities by category, defect rates, and variations from standards. Key stakeholders should determine the breadth and depth of the metric.

Applying change management, therefore, is absolutely crucial to status collection and assessment. You should apply this discipline consistently throughout the project life cycle, to include technical and project management deliverables. The integrity of the cost and schedule baselines must be maintained or the project will fail to achieve the new or revised vision. Baselines, whether for cost, schedule, or scope, or a combination thereof, are critical to a project's success because they give you the means to instill discipline. Unfortunately, few projects actually have a baseline, and it's a sure bet that if you inherit a project in trouble, it very likely did not have any baselines, or maybe only one.

There are several advantages to having baselines:

> One, baselines represent an agreement between a project team and other key stakeholders on meeting specific targets: meeting important schedule dates, adhering to budgetary targets, and handing over specific deliverables to the customer. Failure to exercise due diligence and due care in following baselines is noncompliance with an agreement unless, of course, the customer approves. Hence, penalties for failing to meet specific targets on commercial contracts could be incurred, for example.
>
> Two, baselines provide focus. As your team performs its work, it focuses on the targets that serve as benchmarks telling everyone how well the project is achieving the vision. Scope, cost, and schedule baselines ideally should be integrated.
>
> Three—and this is related to the last point—baselines enable effective management of change. A baseline gives you and your team the ability to see the specific impact of a change from cost, schedule,

and scope perspectives and make rational decisions on whether to approve or disapprove it.

Four, baselines generate useful metrics by providing a comparison between what is planned to occur and what actually has occurred. For example, baselines allow for effective earned value management, comparing planned cost with actual cost performance and indicating whether a variance exists. Without baselines in those two areas, earned value would be impractical.

In essence, baselines impart discipline to your project. All stakeholders work to meet the baselines to work within constraints and stay on track to achieve the vision.

Establishing and maintaining risk management. Identifying potential sources of trouble and developing ways to deal with them is proactive behavior. Similar to the schedule itself, you and your team need to revisit the risks regularly. Visibility of risks and responses to them are essential; otherwise, the vision of the project could find itself in jeopardy.

Building and deploying a communications plan. The plan should identify and satisfy the data and information needs of key stakeholders. It should also allow them to share data and information among themselves. The communications plan should be tied directly to change and risk management. In fact, an argument can be made that good communications management enables good change management and risk management.

An effective communications plan should ensure that the right information gets to the right people in the right format in the right amount at the right time. To do that, it should record who receives the information, when they receive it, how they receive it, why they receive it, and what they receive. Naturally, the communications plan should remain current as stakeholders and circumstances constantly change throughout the project's life cycle.

Monitoring effectiveness. Once you have decided the options to take, you are ready to implement them. You may have put in place all the necessary project management disciplines according to the breadth and depth necessary for the project and are ready to execute them.

Excellent. However, you need to do more. You and your team need to be aware of how well the options chosen are working to turn around your troubled project. Deployment of the option or options is just one step toward successful recovery. You need to collect feedback on the effectiveness of each option. That means applying the Plan-Do-Check-Act (PDCA), or Deming, wheel. The Plan is determining what must be done; you and your team have done that. The Do is executing what was determined to be done; you are and your team are now at that point. Check is having the measures and metrics in place to answer the fundamental question: How well are we doing? Action is making the necessary improvements.

The point here is that your job is not over once you implement the options. You need to keep a pulse on how effective they are and make the necessary adjustments. The selected options are based on the assumptions made and information known at the time; circumstances change, and everyone involved in the recovery of the troubled project needs to be alert to that fact.

6.6 CONCLUSION

Developing a new vision, such as a charter, and building a plan, including a schedule, does not guarantee a successful outcome. It requires key stakeholders to maintain focus on the vision and plan; otherwise, all the efforts expended on the previous actions were merely ornamental, providing little or no value to anyone, least of all to the project.

Project management is about achieving results efficiently and effectively. Unfortunately, sometimes the "fog" of project management clouds perspective and judgment. It is up to the project manager and other stakeholders to ensure that people keep the vision in sight as they deliver the final product on schedule, within budget, and of the highest possible workmanship. You should ensure that good, solid project management disciplines are in place to preclude problems arising that led to your arrival in the first place.

Case Study (*Continued*)

Execute. Deborah now assembled the team for one last planning session before kicking off the project. Deborah decided to have the team take the high-level planning for the STP as a basis for building a more comprehensive plan. During the meeting, she had a project planner with a software tool enter planning information for the schedule. The team referred to a previously generated skills matrix and used it to help construct a responsibility assignment matrix (RAM). Then, people were assigned to work packages in the WBS, and they performed their respective expansion of the elements; they also worked on estimates for their respective assignments.

Deborah decided to implement other project management disciplines with input from the team. These included implementing a change board and a process for managing changes, applying risk management, and building a communications management plan. Because of the visibility and past experience on the project, she implemented earned value management (EVM). She had weekly status collection and reporting, the results being shared with team members and key stakeholders.

One aspect of the communications plan that proved extremely useful was the deployment of a Web site. Although certain content had access restrictions, the Web site served as a powerful medium for sharing and distributing information about the project, both to internal and external team members.

In terms of people issues, Deborah and her management decided to remove Harold from the project. He had boycotted the entire planning process. As the team became increasingly engaged in the planning process, many of members feeling intimidated by him acquired a greater sense of confidence. In fact, throughout the entire project, turnover and absenteeism came to a halt. The team was entirely dedicated to delivering a product on time, within budget, and meeting requirements. All three criteria were met and team members were given bonuses and treated, as a team, to a steak and lobster dinner at a five-star restaurant.

6.7 GETTING-STARTED CHECKLIST

Question	Yes	No
1. When you develop a realistic recovery plan, do you consider the following characteristics of your project:		
Size?	——	——
Execution time?	——	——
Team size?	——	——
Importance?	——	——

Question	Yes	No
Degree of schedule flexibility?	___	___
Risk?	___	___
2. When developing a revised schedule, do you check to ensure that		
All tasks in the schedule are connected with one another?	___	___
All tasks have a start and stop date?	___	___
No task has a TBD (To Be Determined)?	___	___
All dates are based on the work to be done?	___	___
All tasks have someone assigned to perform the work?	___	___
Not all tasks in the schedule are created equal?	___	___
All the tasks appear in the work breakdown structure?	___	___
3. Do you use the skills matrix to assign people to tasks?	___	___
4. Have you created a responsibility assignment matrix (RAM) and distributed it?	___	___
5. Do you use both the skills matrix and the RAM to		
Determine which resource requirements are fulfilled and which ones are lacking?	___	___
Determine lead times to procure the necessary resources to complete tasks?	___	___
Identify sources for procuring missing resources?	___	___
6. Do you get participation and commitment from stakeholders by		
Holding one-on-one plan reviews?	___	___
Holding group plan reviews to resolve integration issues?	___	___
7. Have you determined what you need to do to be persistent and consistent in regard to status collection and assessment?	___	___
8. If you have decided to use earned value management (EVM), have you considered		
How to collect reliable, valid data?	___	___
How to collect data consistently?	___	___
How to collect data regularly?	___	___
What tools to use to generate information?	___	___
How to clearly interpret the information?	___	___
How to make EVM expertise available?	___	___
9. Have you accounted for the following threats to the reliability and validity of data and information:		
Time?	___	___
Measurement?	___	___
Selection?	___	___
Maturation?	___	___
10. If you decide to generate metrics, will you consider		
How it will add value to the customer?	___	___
How it will be based on timely, "clean" data?	___	___
The degree of simplicity?	___	___

Question	Yes	No
11. If implementing change management, will you		
Obtain engagement of key stakeholders?	____	____
Implement change management procedures?	____	____
Recognize that not all changes are equal by setting up an approach for categorization and prioritization?	____	____
Develop metrics regarding changes and their fates?	____	____
12. When implementing risk management, will you apply		
Risk identification?	____	____
Risk assessment, for example, quantitative, qualitative?	____	____
Risk response, for example, strategies?	____	____
Risk reporting?	____	____
13. If developing and deploying a communications management plan, do you identify the		
Audience?	____	____
Medium?	____	____
Topics?	____	____
Frequencies?	____	____
14. When looking at the current schedule for improvement, do you		
Distinguish between hard and soft logic and alter the latter to improve schedule performance?	____	____
Evaluate the practicality of each constraint date?	____	____
Ensure tasks are defined down to a meaningful level to serve as a tool for measuring progress?	____	____
Verify not using planning packages as an excuse for not planning in greater detail?	____	____
Look for incorporating too many burst and merge relationships among tasks, thereby increasing risks?	____	____
Determine if touch points with other projects are affecting performance?	____	____
Employ too many concurrent, or parallel, tasks?	____	____
Ascertain the degree of integration among tasks?	____	____
Check the quality and quantity of resources?	____	____
Look for opportunities to crash the project?	____	____
Verify that all stakeholders, especially team members, understand their assignments?	____	____
After generating histograms for each resource, look for opportunities to level their profiles?	____	____
Ensure that everyone working on a task has given their concurrence to work on it?	____	____
Look at resource allocation on an individual and group perspective?	____	____
When reallocating resources, do you keep these guidelines in mind:	____	____

Question	Yes	No
Give preference to tasks on the critical path?	____	____
For concurrent tasks, give preference to the one with the most negative float or ones with the most complexity?	____	____

7

Final Thoughts

7.1 THE ODDS ARE NOT IN YOUR FAVOR

As a project manager, you have either managed a project that got into trouble or you have inherited one. Either way, the experience is not a pleasant one. The odds are just against you even more so over time.

The approach described in this book will increase your odds of success in turning around any project in trouble. Odds? That's right, odds. The approach does not guarantee success; it does, however, increase your chances of successfully leading such projects.

What has been presented in this book is not a cookie cutter, or paint-by-numbers approach. If that were the case, more projects would become successful simply by following the prescribed steps. Only you can turn around a project; the approach simply gives you a road map for doing so. Each action and its corresponding set of activities described in this book still require judgment on your part in terms of application.

Expect to face, therefore, more gray situations and a few black-and-white ones as you apply the five E's, shown in Figure 7.1. You will make decisions about their application, and you may even make matters worse from time to time. With trial and error, however, you will be able to determine the depth and breadth of each action to apply on your project, a sure sign of a seasoned, professional project manager.

As mentioned in the introduction, all five actions—Energize, Envision, Explore, Evaluate, and Execute—are nonsequential. That is, all five actions and even the activities within them will more often than not occur non-linearly, or nonsequentially. Again, it cannot be overemphasized that this is not a cookie-cutter approach to turning around a project.

Hopefully, you now appreciate why this approach is heavily based on the people side of project management. Although tools and techniques are

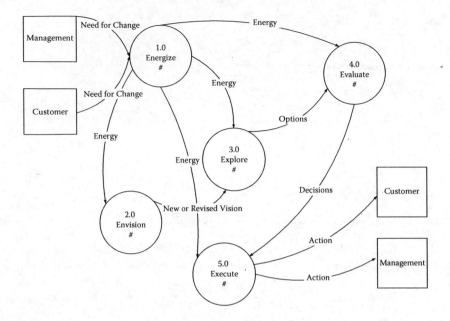

FIGURE 7.1
Level One: Overview.

important, it is the people—individual or organizations (also consisting of people, of course)—who make effective change happen on a project. You can perform tasks such as scheduling and cost estimating, but none of that matters if you don't get the people engaged. You need people to make it all happen, and without their participation and collaboration the project may never get turned around.

7.2 NOW THE 5 Cs

Your engagement of people takes what I call the five C's: Communication, Collaboration, Commitment, Concentration, and Change Management.

Communication is absolutely essential. You learned that project managers communicate more often and with a greater variety of people than most other stakeholders. You, as a project manager, need to communicate both laterally and vertically using media that is conducive to their needs. Your message must be on target. One-on-one and group communications, as discussed earlier, are critical to ensure effective communications. Communication spans all five E's.

Collaboration is key. Working together in an integrative and inter-dependent manner allows for achieving synergistic results. Unless each stakeholder knows the extent of his or her contribution to the work of others and the overall vision, everyone will perform aim-lessly, leading to dissipated energy and disequilibrium. Scheduling and team building are two examples where greater collaboration can occur. Collaboration spans all five E's.

Commitment is key. No one will follow anything unless they have some level of commitment. The same goes for work on a project. People must be emotionally as well as intellectually engaged. Indeed, a strong argument can be made to give preference to the former. You will need to provide the initial spark to obtain the commitment and constantly make an effort to sustain it. Getting stakeholders involved in developing a new or revised vision and a schedule are two prime examples of ways to ensure commitment. Commitment spans all five E's.

Concentration is key. With concentration, all stakeholders direct their attention to what matters: the vision as defined by the customer. Without it, all stakeholders once again can find themselves wander-ing about aimlessly, working hard but failing to move the project forward. With all their energy and effort directed with laser preci-sion toward accomplishing the vision, the team becomes both effec-tive and efficient. Basing all subsequent planning and decisions on the vision effectively ensures concentration. Concentration spans all five E's.

Change Management is key. All projects are about change to one degree or another, and their environments are constantly chang-ing. You need to have a handle on dealing with the latter. In other words, you need to manage change or it will manage you. The last thing you need is to be involved in constant firefights, with you and your team constantly in a defensive, reactive mode; otherwise, you and your team will get in trouble. Next, you and your project will be in trouble. Using the new or revised vision and the input from your team, you have to maintain a pulse on what changes have or may have caused the project to go awry. Change management spans all five E's.

7.3 THE FIVE SECRETS

As the project manager of a troubled project, you face immense pressure. You face pressures from many stakeholders as you try to turn your project into a princess while simultaneously having cost, schedule, and quality constraints imposed on you. At the same time, you are expected to achieve a new or revised vision that had gotten blurry in the past. Fortunately, you now have an approach to increase your odds of success—the five E's: Energize, Envision, Explore, Evaluate, and Execute.

Glossary

Abraham Maslow: Developer of a motivational theory based on a hierarchy of needs, starting with the physiological ones and ending with self-actualization.

Affinity diagram: The process of taking a disparate pile of items and grouping them according to some categorization scheme.

Adjourning phase: The fifth of five phases that a team goes through, in which team members celebrate the achievement of an event.

Aggressive leadership behavior: Negative behavior that forces the achievement of the vision, often through the use of negative incentives.

Applied thinking: A disciplined approach to thinking that requires asking questions such as "How?"

Arbitrary and capricious: Whimsical decision making and taking actions without considering the thoughts, feelings, etc., of stakeholders and the facts and data surrounding the situation under consideration.

Art of project management: The application of critical thinking skills that answers questions such as "Why are we doing this?" and "Is there a better way?" when leading and managing a project.

Assertive leadership behavior: Positive behavior that encourages the achievement of the vision for the project, often using positive incentives.

Assumptions: Suppositions or perceptions that are assumed to be facts until proved otherwise.

Baseline: A target or agreed-upon performance criterion to determine progress relative to actual performance.

Behavioral leadership theory: Using psychological and sociological approaches to motivate team members.

Benchmarking: Comparing an organization with another one to determine ranking and areas for improvement.

Brainstorming: Generating a list of ideas without screening and evaluating them.

Budget: The monies allocated to achieve the vision of the project.

Budget performance: A disciplined approach used to manage the allocation of funding for a project.

Burn-down chart: A physical or conceptual count of artifacts being produced over a period of time; the count continues until all occurrences of a given artifact, for example, a document, are complete.

Business case: A study that demonstrates or disproves the financial value of a project.

Cause and effect graph: A diagram showing the relationships among different causes and their consequences.

Change control log: A detailed listing of changes (to include approved, disapproved, or suspended) that records information about each one.

Change management: A disciplined approach toward recording, evaluating, and tracking changes.

Charter: A high-level document describing the purpose, scope, goals, objectives, risks, constraints, etc. to accomplish the vision of a project mainly from a business perspective.

Chunking: The process of breaking a large component or item into its basic elements to increase understanding and analysis.

Coercive power: One of the five types of power, predicated on fear.

Communication management: A disciplined approach toward managing the generating and dispersing of information.

Communication formula: A calculation that derives the number of communication channels on a team by using the number of people as input.

Compliance: Adherence to laws, regulations, etc.

Consensus: Stakeholders understand, accept, and support a decision or action despite reservations.

Constraints: The conditions that restrict the options of a team.

Core team: A small number of team members serving as the nucleus to accomplish the vision for the project.

Cost: The expenses required to complete a project.

Crashing: Piling resources on the critical path in the expectation of improving schedule performance.

Crawford slip technique: Individuals generate ideas on a note card or slip of paper, which are next compiled and categorized. Then, the list is pruned by eliminating some ideas.

Critical path: The tasks in a schedule that cannot slide without impacting the project completion date.

Critical thinking: A disciplined approach to thinking that seeks to answer questions like "Why?"

Customer: The person or organization for whom the project is building a product or providing a service.

Daily stand-up: A 15-minute information-sharing session for team members.

David McClelland: The developer of the motivational theory based on the premise that people are motivated by a need for power, achievement, or love.

de Bono's hat thinking: Conceptualizing the use of colored hats to reflect different modes of thinking.

Deliverable: The completion of an artifact that will or may result in the delivery of the final product or service to the customer.

Delphi approach: A technique that involves sending a questionnaire to individuals until consensus is achieved.

Disequilibrium: The state of a system whereby it operates in an erratic manner, making it difficult for it to adapt to its environment.

Douglas McGregor: The developer of a motivational theory based on one positive (Theory Y) or negative (Theory X) perspective of people.

Earned Value Management (EVM): A schedule and cost performance management technique that compares and monitors planned and actual outcomes.

Energize: One of the five key actions for turning around a project in trouble; it involves sparking the team toward making significant improvements.

Envision: One of the five key actions for turning around a project in trouble; it involves requiring revisiting the vision and developing a new or revised vision.

Equilibrium: A state of a system whereby it operates at a steady, optimum level of performance.

Evaluate: One of the five key actions for turning around a project in trouble; it involves determining the options that will enable achievement of the vision.

Execute: One of the five key actions for turning around a project in trouble; it involves executing the option or options selected in the Evaluate action.

Expert power: One of the five types of power, based on a person's knowledge and expertise.

Explore: One of the five key actions for turning around a project in trouble; it involves looking at all the options available to execute the new or revised vision.

Fast tracking: The arrangement of many tasks in parallel, or concurrently, within a schedule to compress its timeline.

Forced choice technique: A method that forces participants to select one option over another.

Force field analysis: A technique that involves identifying the pros and cons of an idea.

Forming phase: The first of five phases that a team goes through, whereby team members start to become familiar with each other.

Frederick Herzberg: The developer of a motivational theory based on two sets of needs: satisfiers (primarily psychological) and dissatisfiers (primarily physiological).

Free association: The process of developing a mental connection between two or more concepts, items, etc., to derive a new idea, solution, etc.

Gap analysis: A description of the differences between the proposed vision and what actually exists.

GIGO: An acronym standing for Garbage In, Garbage Out; it means that bad data will generate bad information.

Gold plating: Giving more to the customer than was originally requested.

Group session: The project manager meets with the entire team to obtain information and feedback as well as consensus on issues, challenges, solutions, etc. that could be obtained in a one-on-one session.

Groupthink: A group of people exhibiting such extreme conformity that it results in intolerance of new ideas and an unrealistic appraisal of situations.

Incremental development: Multiple releases of a product or service according to varying degrees of breadth and depth to satisfy customer expectations.

Integrated product teams: A multidisciplinary group of individuals responsible for producing a deliverable that will be incorporated in the final product or service delivered to the customer.

Interviewing: Meeting with one or more individuals to gather information, insights, etc. by asking them questions.

Ishikawa diagram: Also known as the fishbone diagram, this approach involves defining a problem, issue, or challenge and then identifying its causes, usually in four categories: material, manpower, methods, and machines.

Iteration: A subset of a release.

Leading: Using psychological and sociological approaches to enable people to achieve the vision of the project; it involves "doing the right things."

Lean: A manufacturing philosophy consisting of a set of concepts, principles, tools, and practices to improve supply chain performance based on meeting the requirements of the customer.

Legitimate power: One of the five types of power, which is predicated on a person's position within an organization.

Lessons learned: One or more sessions with the objectives of understanding what went well and what areas needed improvement. It is conducted after a major event, such as completing a phase or a project.

Management: The stakeholders who participate in setting the strategic direction of a project.

Management by confusion: A style of management whereby the team members, including the project manager, work in what appears to be an aimless manner, such as often deviating from the vision.

Management by crisis: A style of management whereby the project manager reacts to problems, causes, etc. as they arise.

Management by drives: A style of management whereby the project team starts slowly and then accelerates performance toward the end of a project's life cycle.

Management by effectiveness: A style of management whereby all the project manager's decisions, actions, behavior, etc. focus on furthering the achievement of the vision.

Managing: Applying the concepts and principles of project management as well as the tools and techniques in order to "do things right," for example, building an integrated schedule.

Metric: An indicator based on one or more measurements of cost, schedule, quality, and technical performance of a project.

Mind guards: People who take on the responsibility of being the guardians for a group to reserve or protect its beliefs, values, and mores.

Mind mapping: A technique to generate ideas and reflect their relationships in the form of a neural net.

Modeling: Constructing diagrams that reflect processes, procedures, components of a system, etc. as a way to improve understanding and develop ideas.

Needs: Requirements that must be minimally met by the project.

Net present value: A financial calculation that accounts for the time value of money and is used in determining return on investment.

Nominal group technique: A brainstorming approach that entails generating and categorizing ideas and then voting for the best ones.

Non-value-added work: Tasks and output that do not contribute toward achieving the vision of a project.

Norming phase: The third of five phases that a team goes through, whereby team members have reconciled significant differences and are working together.

One-on-one sessions: The project manager meets separately with each team member to obtain information, feedback, etc. that they would not usually receive in a group session.

Opportunity: A positive risk that, if it occurs, enhances progress.

Ostracism: A person is expelled from a group for various reasons, for example, beliefs, physical characteristics.

Outsourcing: Having vendors, buyers, etc. be responsible for producing part or all the deliverables on a project.

PDCA wheel: An acronym that stands for Plan-Do-Check-Act, meaning that you define your goal or objective, take action to achieve it, measure its effectiveness, and then take corrective action, if necessary.

Performing phase: The fourth of five phases that a team goes through, whereby team members focus on achieving the mission, tolerate new ideas, etc.

Piggybacking: A concept whereby one idea is used as a springboard to generate a related or different idea mentioned earlier.

Portfolio management: An array of projects, programs, and initiatives chosen to accomplish the strategic goals and objectives of an organization.

Prioritization matrix: A four square chart indicating the degree of relationship between two variables.

Procurement management: A disciplined approach toward obtaining and tracking the necessary labor and nonlabor resources for a project.

Product backlog: The incomplete or remaining work that keeps piling up over time.

Project management triangle: A geometric figure displaying the relationships among cost, schedule, and quality; sometimes, scope and risk are also included in the triangle.

Prototype: A model of the final deliverable or service that enables stakeholders to make adjustments to satisfy requirements.

Qualitative risk management: A subjective approach taken to identify, evaluate, and respond to threats and opportunities that could impact a project.

Quality: The standards that the project must meet to be considered correct from a quality assurance perspective.

Quality management: A disciplined approach toward ensuring that the output of a project conforms to the applicable standards and guidelines.

Quantitative risk management: A mathematical approach taken to evaluate and respond to threats and opportunities that could impact a project.

Referent power: One of the five types of power, which is predicated on a person's characteristics, such as personality or physical stature.

Release: A working component or service representing a version of the eventually fully completed deliverable.

Requirements documentation: The criteria for delivering the final product or service to the customer.

Resource allocation: The distribution of resources among the tasks to be executed on a project.

Resource histogram: A set of vertical bars used to reflect the planned and actual usages of labor and nonlabor resources.

Responsibility: The person or organization designated to execute a task or tasks to produce a deliverable.

Responsibility assignment matrix (RAM): A chart showing the assignment and level of responsibility of people assigned to tasks identified in the work breakdown structure (WBS).

Return on investment (ROI): A calculation demonstrating the planned or actual financial gain or loss of a project.

Reward power: One of the five types of power, which is predicated on the capacity to provide rewards.

Risk: Future scenarios or events, positive or negative, which could affect the results of a project.

Risk management: A disciplined approach used to identify future scenarios or events that could positively or negatively impact a project.

Rolling wave concept: Progressive elaboration of a component or plan, for example, as more information becomes known.

Schedule: A road map displaying the sequence and times for accomplishing the vision of a project.

Science of project management: The application of applied thinking skills that involves answering questions such as "How is this done?"

Scope: The result of a project within specifications or requirements; anything not within the specifications or requirements is excluded from being produced.

Scope creep: The gradual, uncontrollable expansion of the features and functions of the product or service being delivered to the customer.

Scope management: A disciplined approach used to identify and focus on the vision for a project.

Situational leadership theory: Adapting one's approach to leadership based on contextual considerations.

Situation-Target-Proposal (STP): A report that explains the current circumstances, the desired end state, and the means to achieve the vision.

Skills matrix: A chart showing the relationship between specific abilities, knowledge, etc. and the extent to which team members satisfy those requirements.

SMART: An acronym often used to describe the characteristics of a goal or objective. It stands for Specific, Measurable, Achievable, Realistic, and Time-Bound, though the letters sometimes stand for something else, depending on the context.

Stakeholder: A person or organization having a direct or indirect interest in the outcome of a project.

Stakeholder log: A medium used to capture information about each stakeholder.

Stakeholder matrix: A chart or diagram displaying the relationship between characteristics about stakeholders, for example, interest and power.

Statement of work: A detailed description, for example, functions and features of the final product or service being delivered to the customer. It is often appended to the charter.

Storming phase: The second of five phases that a team goes through in which team members start identifying and dealing with differences related to rules, responsibilities, authorities, etc.

Storyboarding: A technique for defining a problem or challenge and addressing it from the perspective of four areas: planning, ideas, organization, and communications.

Synectics: A group leader states a problem that the team in turn restates and then generates ideas for improvement based on the use of analogies.

Systems approach: Taking a holistic perspective that not only involves looking at the components of a system but their relationships, too.

TANSTAAFL: An acronym standing for There Ain't No Such Thing As A Free Lunch, meaning nothing occurs without an impact of some sort, positive or negative.

Threat: A negative risk that, if it occurs, will retard progress.

Time-out: A respite to slow the momentum of a project so that people address the challenges, issues, problems, etc. confronting a project.

Trait leadership theory: The physical qualities of people as a basis for leading.

Transformational leadership: An approach to leading in which the leader causes the team to progress to a higher level of performance.

Transactional leadership: An approach to leading in which the leader has the team focus on doing business as usual, thereby not taking the project to a higher level of performance.

Tuchman model: A five (originally four) phase model describing the various conditions that a typical team goes through.

Virtual team: A team in which the participants are not physically co-located but interact with each other through electronic media.

Vision: A technical and business description of the final product or service being delivered to the customer.

Visualization: Imagining the functions, features, performance, and other characteristics of the final product or service. The emphasis is on how it should be and is, therefore, prescriptive.

Wants: Requirements that are nice to have; that is, they are not necessary to achieve the vision of the project but would please the customer.

Weighting options table: A display of options with relative weights indicating the degree to which an option satisfies requirements.

WIIFM: An acronym that stands for What's In It For Me. It means that people don't do anything unless some personal need will be satisfied.

Win-lose outcome: A relationship that results in one party gaining and the other one losing. An example is a negotiation in which one party wins and the other one loses.

Win-win outcome: A relationship that results in a mutually satisfying gain for both parties. An example is a negotiation in which both parties feel they've achieved their goals.

Work breakdown structure (WBS): A hierarchical decomposition of a deliverable or deliverables and tasks or subtasks on a project.

Bibliography

Ackoff, Russell L. *The Art of Problem Solving.* New York: John Wiley & Sons, 1978.

Adams, James L. *Conceptual Blockbusting: A Guide to Better Idea Ideas.* 2nd ed., New York: W. W. Norton and Company, 1979.

Armstrong, Thomas. *7 Kinds of Smarts.* New York: Plume, 1993.

Baker, Sunny, Baker, Kim, and Campbell, G. Michael. *The Complete Idiot's Guide to Project Management.* 3rd ed. New York: Alpha, 2003.

Barkley, Bruce T. and Saylor, James H. *Customer-Driven Project Management.* New York: McGraw-Hill, 2001.

Bellman, Geoffrey M. *Getting Things Done When You Are Not in Charge.* San Francisco: Berrett-Koehler, 1992.

Birkman, Roger. *True Colors.* Nashville, TN: Thomas Nelson, Inc., 1997.

Block, Robert. *The Politics of Projects.* New York: Yourdon Press, 1983.

Bramson, Robert M. *Coping with Difficult People.* New York: Dell, 1981.

Brassard, Michael. *The Memory Jogger Plus+ Featuring the Seven Management Planning Tools.* Methuen, MA: GOAL/QPC, 1989.

Brassard, Michael and Ritter, Diane. *The Memory Jogger II: A Pocket Guide of Tools for Continuous Improvement and Effective Planning.* Metheun, MA: GOAL/QPC, 1994.

Briner, Wendy, Geddes, Michael, and Hastings, Colin. *Project Leadership.* Aldershot: Gower, 1990.

Buzan, Tony. *Use Both Sides of Your Brain.* New York: E. P. Dutton, 1983.

Cook, Marshall J. *Effective Coaching.* New York: McGraw-Hill, 1999.

De Bono, Edward. *Atlas of Management Thinking.* Middlesex, England: Pelican Books, 1983.

De Bono, Edward. *Lateral Thinking: Creativity Step-by-Step.* New York: Harper & Row, 1990.

De Bono, Edward. *Practical Thinking.* London: Penguin Books, 1991.

De Bono, Edward. *Six Thinking Hats.* Boston: Little, Brown and Company, 1985.

De Bono, Edward. *The Use of Lateral Thinking.* London: Penguin Books, 1990.

Demarco, Tom and Lister, Timothy. *Peopleware: Productive Projects and Teams.* New York: Dorset House Publishing Co., 1987.

Dinsmore, Paul C. and Cabanis-Brewin, Jeannette, Eds., The *AMA Handbook of Project Management.* 2nd ed. New York: Amacom, 2006.

Doyle, Michael and Straus, David. *How to Make Meetings Work.* New York: Jove Books, 1976.

Driver, Michael J., Brousseau, Kenneth R., and Hunsaker, Phillip L. *The Dynamic Decision Maker: Five Decision Styles for Executives and Business Success.* San Francisco: Jossey-Bass, 1993.

Flannes, N. and Levin, Ginger. *Essential People Skills for Project Managers.* Vienna, VA: Management Concepts, 2005.

Fleming, Quentin. *Cost/Schedule Control Systems Criteria.* Chicago: Probus Publishing Company, 1992.

Fleming, Quentin and Koppelman, Joel M. *Earned Value Project Management.* 2nd ed. Newtown Square, PA: Project Management Institute, 2000.

Fox, William M. *Effective Group Problem Solving.* San Francisco: Jossey-Bass Publishers, 1990.

Freedman, Daniel and Weinberg, Gerald M. *Handbook of Walkthroughs, Inspections, and Technical Reviews.* New York: Dorset House Publishing, 1990.

Gardner, Howard. *Multiple Intelligences: The Theory in Practice.* New York: Basic Books, 1993.

Gebelein, Susan et al. *Successful Manager's Handbook.* North America: Personnel Decisions International, 2000.

Gido, Jack and Clements, James P. *Successful Project Management.* Cincinnati, OH: South-Western College Publishing, 1999.

Glass, Robert L. *Computing Failure.com: War Stories from the Electronic Revolution.* Upper Saddle River, NJ: Prentice Hall PTR, 2001.

Glass, Peter L. *Software Runaways.* Upper Saddle River, NJ: Prentice Hall PTR, 1998.

Goleman, Daniel, Kaufman, Paul, and Ray, Michael. *The Creative Spirit.* New York: Dutton, 1992.

Grady, Robert B. *Practical Software Metrics for Project Management and Process Improvement.* Englewood Cliffs, NJ: Prentice Hall, 1992.

Graham, Robert J. and Englund, Randall L. *Creating an Environment for Successful Projects.* San Francisco: Jossey-Bass, 1997.

Guy, Dan M. and Carmichael, D. R. *Audit Sampling: An Introduction to Statistical Sampling in Auditing.* 2nd ed. New York: John Wiley & Sons, 1986.

Harvard Business Review. *Managing Projects and Programs.* Boston: Harvard Business School Press, 1989.

Higgins, James M. 101 *Creative Problem Solving Techniques: The Handbook of New Ideas for Business.* Winter Park, FL: The New Management Publishing Company, 1994.

Hunter, Dale, Bailey, Anne, and Taylor, Bill. *The Art of Facilitation.* Cambridge, MA: Fisher Books, 1995.

Juran, J. M. *Juran's Quality Control Handbook.* 4th ed. New York: McGraw-Hill Book Company, 1988.

Karrass, Chester L. *The Negotiating Game.* New York: Thomas Y. Crowell Company, 1970.

Keane, Inc. *Productivity Management.* 2nd ed. Boston: Keane, Inc., 1995.

Kerzner, Harold. *Strategic Planning for Project Management Using a Project Management Maturity Model.* New York: John Wiley & Sons, 2001.

Kerzner, Harold. *Project Management: A Systems Approach to Planning, Scheduling, and Controlling.* 9th ed. Hoboken, NJ: John Wiley & Sons, 2006.

Kliem, Ralph L. *Effective Communications for Project Management.* Boca Raton, FL: Auerbach, 2008.

Kliem, Ralph L. *Leading High-Performance Projects.* Boca Raton, FL: J. Ross Publishing, 2004.

Kliem, Ralph L. *The Project Manager's Emergency Kit.* Boca Raton, FL: St. Lucie Press, 2003.

Kliem, Ralph. *The Secrets of Successful Project Management.* New York: John Wiley & Sons, 1986.

Kliem, Ralph L. and Anderson, Harris B. *The Organizational Engineering Approach to Project Management.* Boca Raton, FL: St. Lucie Press, 2003.

Kliem, Ralph L. and Ludin, Irwin S. *Reducing Project Risk.* Aldershot: Gower, 1997.

Kliem, Ralph L. and Ludin, Irwin S. *The Noah Project.* Aldershot: Gower, 1993.

Kliem, Ralph L. and Ludin, Irwin S. *The People Side of Project Management.* Aldershot: Gower, 1992.

Kliem, Ralph L. and Ludin, Irwin S. *Tools and Tips for Today's Project Manager.* Newtown Square, PA: Project Management Institute, 1999.

Kliem, Ralph L., Ludin, Irwin S., and Robertson, Ken L. *Project Management Methodology: A Practical Guide to the Next Millennium.* New York: Marcel Dekker, 1997.

Lejk, Mark and Deeks, David. *An Introduction to Systems Analysis Techniques.* 2nd ed. Harlow, England: Addison-Wesley, 2002.

Levi, Daniel. *Group Dynamics for Teams.* Thousand Oaks, CA: Sage Publications, 2001.

Lewis, James P. *Project Leadership*. New York: McGraw Hill, 2003.

Lewis, James P. *The Project Manager's Desk Reference*. Chicago: Irwin Professional Publishing, 1995.

Lewis, James P. *Project Planning Scheduling and Control*. 3rd ed. New York: McGraw-Hill, 2000.

Martin, Paula and Tate, Karen. *Project Management Memory Jogger: A Pocket Guide for Project Teams*. Salem, NH: GOAL/QPC, 1997.

McNamee, Peter and Celona, John. *Decision Analysis for Professionals*. 3rd ed. Menlo Park, CA: SmartOrg, Inc., 2001.

Merrill, David W. and Reid, Roger H. *Personal Styles and Effective Performance*. Radnor, PA: Chilton Book Company, 1981.

Meredith, Jack R. and Mantel, Samuel J., Jr. *Project Management: A Managerial Approach*. 2nd ed. New York: John Wiley & Sons, 1989.

Mersino, Anthony. *Emotional Intelligence for Project Managers*. New York: Amacom, 2007.

Metzger, Philip and Boddie, John. *Managing a Programming Project: Processes and People*. 3rd ed. Upper Saddle River, NJ: Prentice Hall, 1996.

Newell, Michael W. *Preparing for the Project Management Professional (PMP) Certification Exam*. New York: Amacom, 2001.

Nierenberg, Gerard I. *The Art of Creative Thinking*. New York: Cornerstone Library, 1982.

Nierenberg, Gerard I. *The Art of Negotiating*. New York: Cornerstone Library, 1979.

Nierenberg, Gerard I. *The Complete Negotiator*. New York: Nierenberg and Zeif Publishers, 1986.

Nirenberg, Jesse. *Getting Through to People*. Englewood Cliffs, NJ: Prentice-Hall, 1963.

O'Connell, Fergus. *How to Run Successful Projects II*. London: Prentice Hall, 1994.

Olson, Jeff. *The Agile Manager's Guide to Giving Great Presentations*. Bristol, VT: Velocity Business Publishing, 1997.

Palmer, Helen. *The Enneagram: Understanding Yourself and the Others*. New York: HarperSanFrancisco, 1991.

Pickering, Peg. *How to Handle Conflict and Confrontation*. Shawnee Mission, KS: National Press Publications, 2000.

Poppendieck, Mary and Poppendieck, Tom. *Implementing Lean Software Development*. Upper Saddle River, NJ: Addison-Wesley, 2007.

Riso, Don R. *Personality Types: Using the Enneagram for Self-Discovery*. Boston: Houghton Mifflin Company, 1990.

Rotondo, Jennifer and Rotondo, Fr., Mike. *Presentation Skills for Managers*. New York: McGraw-Hill, 2002.

Rutman, Leonard, ed., *Evaluation Research Methods: A Basic Guide*. Beverly Hills, CA: Sage Publications, 1977.

Sagan, Carl. *The Demon-Haunted World*. New York: Ballantine Books, 1997.

Schwalbe, Kathy. *Information Technology Project Management*. Cambridge, MA: Course Technology, 2000.

Sliger, Michele and Broderick, Stacia. *The Software Project Manager's Bridge to Agility*. Upper Saddle River, NJ: Addison-Wesley, 2008.

Straub, Joseph T. *The Agile Manager's Guide to Building and Leading Teams*. Bristol, VT: Velocity Business Publishing, 1998.

Straub, Joseph T. *The Agile Manager's Guide to Motivating People*. Bristol, VT: Velocity Business Publishing, 1997.

Tieger, Paul D. and Barron-Tieger, Barbara. *Do What You Are*. Boston: Little, Brown and Company, 2001.

Tubbs, Stewart L. *A Systems Approach to Small Group Interaction.* 6th ed. Boston: McGraw-Hill, 1998.

Tubbs, Stewart L. and Moss, Sylvia. *Human Communication.* 8th ed. Boston: McGraw-Hill, 2000.

Vance, Mike and Deacon, Diane. *Think Out of the Box.* Franklin Lakes, NJ: Career Press, 1997.

VanGundy, Arthur B. *Creative Problem Solving: A Guide for Trainers and Management.* New York: Quorum Books, 1987.

Verma, Vijay K. *Human Resource Skills for the Project Manager.* Newtown Square, PA: Project Management Institute, 1996.

Von Oech, Roger. *A Whack on the Side of the Head: How You Can Be More Creative.* New York: Warner Books, 1990.

Ward, J. Leroy. *Project Management Terms: A Working Glossary.* Arlington, VA: ESI International, 1999.

Wonder, Jacquelyn and Donovan, Priscilla. *Whole-Brain Thinking: Working with Both Sides of the Brain.* New York: Quill, 1984.

Wysocki, Robert K., Beck, Jr., Robert., and Crane, David B. *Effective Project Management.* 2nd ed. New York: John Wiley & Sons, 2000.

Index